D1128716

Perception, Expression, and History

John O'Neill

Perception, Expression, and History

*The Social Phenomenology
of Maurice Merleau-Ponty*

NORTHWESTERN UNIVERSITY PRESS
EVANSTON   1 9 7 0

John O'Neill is Associate Professor of Sociology at
York University, Toronto, Ontario. He has translated
*Themes from the Lectures at the Collège de France,
1952–1960* and *Humanism and Terror,*
both by Merleau-Ponty.

For my father and mother
who gave me a name, and
a home, and a faith.

Contents

Preface   /   **ix**

   1   /   The Structures of Behavior   /   3
   2   /   The Phenomenology of Perception   /   13
   3   /   Phenomenology in the Natural
             Attitude   /   20
   4   /   Corporeality and Intersubjectivity   /   36
   5   /   Institution, Language, and
             Historicity   /   46
   6   /   Between Montaigne and
             Machiavelli   /   65

Bibliography   /   **90**

Preface

IN THIS BOOK I have been selective in the themes which I have brought together, and I have tried to keep to the style of Merleau-Ponty's thought and language. I am aware that critical discussion of Merleau-Ponty's work is steadily mounting in the journals, but I have preferred to stick to commentary. I have concentrated upon three themes in the goal that Merleau-Ponty set himself, namely, to "restore to things their concrete physiognomy, to organisms their individual ways of dealing with the world, and to subjectivity its inherence in history." [1] These three objectives are considered here in their original order: first, the study of animal and human psychology; then, the phenomenology of perception; and finally, certain extensions of these perspectives in the

1. M. Merleau-Ponty, *Phenomenology of Perception,* trans. Colin Smith (London: Routledge and Kegan Paul; New York: Humanities Press, 1962), p. 57.

historical and social sciences. Of course, Merleau-Ponty ordinarily works upon all these levels in any given study, and this is natural to the broader framework of his task, which is, as he puts it, "to see rationalism in a historical perspective which it set itself on principle to avoid, to seek a philosophy which explains the upsurge of reason in a world not of its making and to prepare the substructure of living experience without which reason and liberty are emptied of their content and wither away." [2]

I am grateful to York University, to Dean John T. Saywell, chairman of the Committee on Minor Research Grants, and to Professor Frederick Elkin, chairman of the Department of Sociology, for their support and the freedom they afforded me to take advantage of generous Awards from The Canada Council in the summers of 1966 and 1967. In Paris I had the privilege of discussing the outline of my study with Madame Merleau-Ponty, Monsieur Jean-Paul Sartre, the late Professor Jean Hyppolite, and Professors Jean Wahl and Claude Lefort. In Louvain I was warmly received by the Reverend H. L. van Breda, director of the Husserl Archives, who in every way facilitated the consultation of Husserlian manuscripts studied by Merleau-Ponty.

It would be false to the sense of this study if the recognition of the support of institutions, colleagues, friends and family and, most of all, the exchanges which grow between oneself and the thought of an author like Merleau-Ponty, were noted in a hurried courtesy.

2. *Ibid.*, pp. 56–57.

Over a period of time a book brings together many lives, borrowing from each in so many ways until it is no longer possible to separate the exigency and the gift which unites them. Merleau-Ponty has taught me to understand the philosophical life apart from its posture of loneliness. "I borrow myself from others; I create others from my own thoughts. This is no failure to perceive others; it is the perception of others." The study of Merleau-Ponty is no retreat from the world because his thought is an inexhaustible digging at the roots of our inherence in the world, nature and history.

"Philosophy is nature in us, the others in us, and we in them." That is why, when I remember what I owe to all those who shared in bringing this book into the world and to the world itself on warm and rainy days in Paris and Louvain, in the libraries of the Sorbonne and the Collège de France, and on quiet evenings in the Appenzellerstube, I am richer than before and only wish I had more to offer in return.

JOHN O'NEILL

Perception, Expression, and History

1 / The Structures
of Behavior

MERLEAU-PONTY'S ANALYSIS of the structures of behavior proceeds by means of a critical
confrontation of the realism of traditional psychology and physiology with a psychology of form whose
implicit naturalism is likewise rejected.[1] The Gestalt
critique of the constancy hypothesis,[2] if properly

1. Merleau-Ponty's method is the result of his reflections
upon Husserl's critique of psychologism and his own interpretation of Gestalt psychology. "Husserl was really seeking,
largely unknown to himself, a notion like that of the
Gestaltists—the notion of an order of meaning which does
not result from the application of spiritual activity to an
external matter." Cf. "Phenomenology and the Sciences of
Man," in M. Merleau-Ponty, *The Primacy of Perception, and
Other Essays*, ed. James M. Edie (Evanston, Ill.: Northwestern University Press, 1964), p. 72.
2. "The attack of the constancy-hypothesis carried to its
logical conclusion assumes the value of a genuine "phenomenological reduction" (*Phenomenology of Perception*,
p. 47); but A. Gurwitsch, *The Field of Consciousness* (Pittsburgh: Duquesne University Press, 1964), pt. 3, § 4, "The

interpreted, means that the sensible configuration
of an object is not a datum of immediate experience; what is immediate is the meaning or structure
of the object correlative with the "articulation and
melodic unity of my behavior." The meaning of an
object is revealed as a possibility which is only ac-
tualized as being-in-the-world when inserted into a
certain conduct which distributes functional values
according to the demands of the total configuration.

The aim of physiological psychology is to describe a topography without norms or intentionality,
as in the classical theory of reflex behavior. However, once one attempts to make the notions of stimulus, receptor and reflex arc more precise, this aspi-
ration of reflex theory recedes and is salvageable
only by appeal to mechanisms of inhibition and
control.[3] For example, an increasing and continuous
stimulation of the concha in the ear of a cat does
not produce responses according to a continuous
diffusion of excitation through pre-established, continuous motor circuits, as would be expected accord-

Phenomenological Interpretation of the Dismissal of the
Constancy-Hypothesis," considers that this leads only to an
incipient phenomenological reduction.

   3. K. Goldstein, *Human Nature in the Light of Psychopathology* (New York: Schocken Books, 1963), chap. 5.
C. Taylor, *The Explanation of Behavior* (New York: Humanities Press, 1964), p. 270, concludes that "S-R theory is
rich in such question-begging special hypotheses, merely
verbal solutions which leave the problem untouched—'con-
ditional' cues, relative stimuli, sensory integration, acquired
drives of all sorts—which are usually a symptom of a
theory's ill-health."

ing to classical reflex theory.[4] The reactions of the
cat are in sequence: movements of the neck and
front ipsilateral paw, movements of the back ipsilateral paw, contractions of the muscles of the tail
and the torso, movements of the contralateral back
paw and movements of the front contralateral paw.
The significance of the elaboration of the response
is that it is distributed according to the vital movements of the animal rather than according to the
anatomical distribution of the motor impulses. In
other words, everything happens so as to maintain
the upright position of the animal, or "to release a
gesture endowed with biological meaning." In a cu-
rious way, the case of "experimental neurosis" induced in one of Pavlov's dogs through repeated experiments forces upon the theory of conditioned
reflexes the recognition of a pathological behavior
induced through the restriction of a biologically
meaningful environment for the animal.[5] To summarize the first order of behavioral structure, we
may say that *physiology cannot be conceptualized
without biology.*

In his treatment of the central sector of the
nervous system and the classical theory of localiza-
tions, Merleau-Ponty frames his discussion in terms
of Buytendijk's question whether, in dealing with
nerve phenomena, we are dealing in reality "with
functions of the structure or with functional

4. M. Merleau-Ponty, *The Structure of Behavior,* trans.
A. L. Fisher (Boston: Beacon Press, 1963), p. 25.
5. *Ibid.,* p. 23.

structures." [6] The implications of this approach
emerge in the study of pathological behavior, where
what is impaired is not so much the content of
behavior but rather its structural functions, what
Gelb and Goldstein [7] refer to as the "categorial attitude," or Head's [8] power of "symbolic expression."
For example, a patient may be able to "name"
(pseudo-naming, i.e. a simple association of a word
with an object) a "bread knife," an "apple parer," a
"pencil sharpener," and "knife and fork" whenever a
knife is present with the associated objects but be
quite unable to name the "knife" in a categorial
sense, that is to say, to assume an abstract attitude
toward it. Now, as Goldstein points out, this loss of
the abstract term is a general behavior change: "To
have sounds *in an abstract meaning as symbols for
ideas means the same concerning language as to
have the possibility of approaching the world in
general in abstract attitude.*" [9] Furthermore, the patient's substitution of concrete speech behavior cannot be simply identified as a symptom of an impaired speech function without knowledge of the

6. F. Buytendijk, "Über die akustische Wahrnehmung
des Hundes," *Archives néerlandaise de psychologie,* XVII
(1933), 267, quoted in *The Structure of Behavior,* p. 61.

7. K. Goldstein and A. Gelb, "Analysis of a Case of
Figural Blindness," in *A Source Book of Gestalt Psychology,*
ed. W. D. Ellis (London: Routledge and Kegan Paul, 1955),
pp. 315–25.

8. H. Head, *Aphasia and Kindred Disorders of Speech*
(New York: Macmillan, 1926).

9. K. Goldstein, *Language and Language Disturbances*
(New York: Grune and Stratton, 1960), p. 63.

total situation in which the patient's reactions occur. The suppression of the abstract attitude towards the knife might, in the case described, involve behavior designed to handle anxiety about that instrument, which would then indicate the real status —i.e. the functional structure—of the speech behavior.

The nervous system distributes spatial, chromatic, and motor values in a system of transformations which demands that the physiological processes involved be understood by starting from "phenomenal givens." The point of view of conditioned-reflex theory is to consider these systematic transformations as a sum of local transformations, localizable in each point of the cortex by the conditioning effect of the stimulus. But in the case where I put on my coat, thrusting my left arm into the right sleeve that faces me as I go to put it on, there occurs a transformation of spatial indices which, far from depending upon the retinal stimulus as such, depends upon a constellation of both proprioceptive and exteroceptive stimuli. Thus the apparent position of my coat and its virtual variations involved in the course of putting it on must be a function of two variables: the afferent ocular excitations and the ensemble of excitations which represent the current position of my body in the cerebral cortex, changes in the spatial field being a function of my body schema. "Each perceived position has a meaning only as integrated into a framework of space which includes not only a sensible sector, actually perceived, but also a 'virtual space' of which the sensible sector is only a momentary aspect." [10] The structure of behavior involved in putting on my coat involves an integration of two distinct constitutive layers, the physiological process of grasping concrete space in the visual field, and the normal perceptual behavior which integrates concrete space into a virtual space. To summarize the second order of behavioral structure, we may say that *physiology cannot be conceptualized without psychology*.

On the basis of his critique of the reductionism and elementarism of behavioral theory, Merleau-Ponty proposes to classify behavior according to a continuum whose upper and lower limits are defined by the submergence of the structure of behavior in content, at the lowest level, to where structure emerges at the highest level as the proper theme of activity. One might then distinguish three levels of behavior—"syncretic forms," "amovable forms," and "symbolic forms"—present in varying degrees in all animal and human behavior. In the simplest syncretic forms of behavior the responses of the organism are, so to speak, total for a specific vital situation rather than drawn from a variable repertoire which would involve the use of *signals* not determined by the organism's instinctual equipment. It is in the amovable forms, or higher animal behavior, that reactions are structured in accordance with the

10. *The Structure of Behavior,* p. 90.

perception of space-time relationships. This is not merely a question of perception by means of *de facto* contiguities of space and time, as is shown by Koehler's chicken experiments, but involves responses as a relation between relations (Sign-Gestalt).[11] But in the case of animals, space-time and means-end relationships are not purely abstract significations that can regulate behavior as at the human level. Koehler's chimpanzee, when presented with fruit separated from it by the vertical sides of a box, is unable to move the fruit toward the open end of the box in order to get at it, despite the fact that it will make a detour to retrieve fruit thrown outside a window. For the chimpanzee the goal (fruit) is the fixed point and his body is the mobile point. He is unable to exchange these functions so as to make his body the fixed point and the fruit a movable object. "What is really lacking in the animal is the symbolic behavior which it would have to possess in order to find an invariant in the external object, under the diversity of its aspects, comparable to the immediately given invariant of the body proper and in order to treat, reciprocally, its own body as an object among objects." [12] The chimpanzee lacks the symbolic behavior through which the thing-structure becomes possible.

11. W. Koehler, "Simple Structural Functions in the Chimpanzee and in the Chicken," in *A Source Book of Gestalt Psychology*, pp. 217–27.
12. *The Structure of Behavior*, p. 118.

In animal behavior signs remain signals dependent upon empirical associations and never become symbols of true signs in which the representation of the signified is not a relation of correspondence but of expression and orientation towards the virtual. The expression of significations is thematic, as, for example, in the case of the organist who can play a passage without being able to designate separately each key which corresponds to a note. The correlations of visual stimuli and motor excitations are achieved only as transition points in an ensemble of signification which is not a function of the associated visual and motor structures but the reason for their integration. We do not say that the behavior of playing the organ *has* a signification, it *is* itself signification. The organist does not play in objective space but in an expressive space. "In reality his movements during rehearsal are consecratory gestures: they draw effective vectors, discover emotional sources, and create a space of expressiveness as the movements of the augur delimit the templum." [13]

Human behavior, which is essentially symbolic behavior, unfolds through structures or gestures which are not in objective space and time, like physical objects, nor in a purely internal dimension of consciousness, which would be foreign to the world. Merleau-Ponty's analysis and integration of the structures of behavior avoids the dualism of objectivism and subjectivism through a conceptualization

13. *Phenomenology of Perception,* pp. 145–46.

of the body-organism as a mode of being-in-the-world or belonging in the world through its openness to the solicitation of the world. "The world, inasmuch as it harbors living beings, ceases to be a material plenum consisting of juxtaposed parts; it opens up at the place where behavior appears." [14]

The conceptualization of behavior requires the category of Form in order to differentiate the structures of quantity, order and value or signification as the relatively dominant characteristics of matter, life and mind and at the same time relativize the participation of these structures in a hierarchy of forms. Form is not itself an element in the world but a limit toward which biophysical and psychobiological structures tend. In other words, the analysis of form is not a question of the composition of real structures but of the perception of wholes. In a given environment each organism exhibits a preferred mode of behavior which is not the simple sum or function of its milieu and its internal organization but is determined by its general attitude to the world.[15] Through the notion of signification, or coordination by meaning, it is possible to take into account the fact that the organism modifies its milieu in accordance with the internal norms of its activity, while avoiding any notion of vitalism or the

14. *The Structure of Behavior*, p. 125.
15. K. Goldstein, *Human Nature in the Light of Psychopathology*, p. 174, emphasizes that the term *preferred behavior* "does not imply any conscious awareness or choice of a special way of performing; it is merely descriptive of the observable type of behavior."

constitutive activity of the norm upon structure. The organism is a *phenomenal body* in the Kantian sense of a unity of signification in which environment and response are polarities in the same structure of behavior.

2 / The Phenomenology of Perception

"THE THEORY OF THE BODY IMAGE is, implicitly, a theory of perception." The phenomenal body is the matrix of human existence. It is the center around which the world is given as a correlate of its activities. Through the phenomenal body we are open to a world of objects as polarities of bodily action. The phenomenal body is a modality of being-in-the-world which is privileged because it is the archimedean point of action and neither a passive agency of sensory perception nor an obstacle to idealist knowledge. Ordinarily, in the sense that philosophical psychology is implicitly dualist, consciousness is defined as the possession of an object of thought or as transparence to itself and action is defined as a series of events external to each other; consciousness and action are juxtaposed or set in a relation of speculative hierarchy. "Whether consciousness be continuous duration or a center of judgments, in either case this pure activity is without structure, without nature. Correlatively, perception and action taken in that which is specific to them, that is, as the knowledge and modification of reality, are rejected from consciousness." It is the task of a phenomenological description of perception to reveal the structures of knowledge and action in which consciousness is engaged by virtue of its incarnation or embodiment through which it experiences the solicitation of the world and its own activity upon its surroundings (*Umwelt*).

The "I am" is, as Alphonse de Waelhens puts it, a rhetorical affirmation of my belonging to the realm of being. Not that I situate myself among objects in a way analogous to the juxtapositions which obtain between things. For I cannot speak of these physical relations as external to me without instituting a relation of exteriority between myself and my body. Such indeed is the epistemological model of physical science. The latter suppresses the immediacy of the mind-body relation and constructs an abstract epistemological subject whose sole function is to survey a field of physical objects and relations. A phenomenological psychology rejects the subject-object dualism because it retrieves an ontological and epistemological unity prior to the disjunctions of natural science. The status of my body is privileged. I can never be detached from it, not even in the attitude of objectivity. "To say that it is always near me, always there for me, is to say that it is never really in front of me, that I cannot array it before my eyes, that it remains marginal to all my perceptions, that it is *with* me."[1] My body is the vantage point from which I perceive all possible objects. It is my body which is the vehicle of my perception and movement in the world. In neither case is the spatiality and the motility of the body geometric or discrete. The body is the schema of my world, it is the source of an abstract movement or projection which "carves out within that plenum of the world in which concrete movement takes place a zone of reflection and subjectivity: it superimposes upon physical space a potential or human space."[2]

Thus, to take an illustration from Merleau-Ponty, for the player on the field the football field is not an "object" but a field of forces, vectors, and openings which call for "moves" in accordance with the play. The player is not a consciousness surveying the field as a datum; the field is present only as "the immanent term of his practical intentions" and the lines of force in it are continuously restructured with his moves in the course of the game, "the player becomes one with it and feels the direction of the 'goal,' for example, just as immediately as the vertical and horizontal planes of his own body."[3] The player "knows" where the goal is in a manner which is "lived" rather than known, that is to say, in the order of "naturizing thought which internally subtends the characteristic structure of objects."[4]

1. *Phenomenology of Perception*, p. 90.
2. *Ibid.*, p. 111.
3. *The Structure of Behavior*, p. 168.
4. *Ibid.*, p. 199.

In order to characterize the openness of objects to perceptual consciousness and the structures of signification that distinguish them from appearances, Merleau-Ponty proposes to call the objects of perception "phenomena." Consequently, insofar as philosophy is an inventory of consciousness as the milieu of the universe, philosophy becomes a phenomenology whose mark is an inescapable existential index. The objects of perception are not closed entities whose structural laws are known to us *a priori,* but "open, inexhaustible systems which we recognize through a certain style of development." The phenomenon of perspective reveals a synthesis of immanence and transcendence which contains the ambiguity of perception. For the perceived thing exists only insofar as I perceive it, and yet its being is never exhausted by the view I have of it. It is this simultaneous presence and absence that is required for "something" to be perceived at all. The sequence of perspectives that we have of a cube is not a logical transition synthesized by a geometrical hypothesis, but "a kind of practical synthesis"—what Husserl called a "synthesis of identification" in which I anticipate the unseen side of the lamp because I can manipulate it. "One phenomenon releases another, not by means of some objective efficient cause, like those which link together natural events, but by the meaning which it holds out— there is an underlying reason for a thing which guides the flow of phenomena without being explicitly laid down in any one of them, *a sort of operative reason.*" [5]

We understand the world and the objects it presents to us in a kind of symbiosis in which the object's color or tactile quality solicits our being and presents it with a question whose answer is discovered in following the perspectives of the object through in accordance with a symbolism that links each of the sensory qualities of the object. The vehicle of these symbolic interrelations between things or aspects of things is our body, upon which the world exerts a magnetic attraction; "the whole of nature is the setting of our own life, or our interlocutor in a sort of dialogue." To possess a body that is capable of intersensory synergy is to possess a universal setting or schema for all possible styles or typical structures in the natural world, not in accordance with the invariable formula of a *facies totius universi* but as a temporal synthesis of horizons implicit in intentionality. "For us the perceptual synthesis is a temporal synthesis, and subjectivity, at the level of perception, is nothing but temporality, and that is what enables us to leave to the subject of perception his opacity and historicity." [6] The unity of the object is foreshadowed by its qualities just as the object itself is the outline of the world and the unity of the world invokes the unity of the *cogito.*

5. *Phenomenology of Perception*, p. 50, italics added.
6. *Ibid.*, p. 239.

The *cogito* of which Merleau-Ponty speaks is not the *spoken cogito*, or the one which is the subject of discourse and essential truth, but a *tacit cogito,* that is, "myself experienced by myself." [7] This subjectivity does not constitute its world, for it has only a precarious grasp upon a world in which it finds itself "like that of the infant at its first breath, or of the man about to drown and who is impelled towards life." This tacit subjectivity only becomes a *cogito* through its articulation in speech and the perceptual exploration and symbolization of the total logic of the world presupposed by the tacit *cogito.* The logic of the world and subjectivity is neither sequent nor synthetic. It is a "living cohesion" in which I belong to myself while belonging to the world. Pascal's remark, that in one way we understand the world and in another it understands us, presents the possibility of avoiding the antitheses of idealism and realism if we understand that these are one and the same understandings. I understand the world because there is for me near and far, foreground and horizon, and hence a landscape in which things can appear and acquire significance. And this is because my subjectivity is in the world through the body which is the original source of perspective and the possibility of situations. For a disembodied spirit or transcendental subjectivity there can be no perspective, and, far from everything appearing explicitly to such a consciousness, everything would cease to be, for such a

7. *Ibid.,* p. 403.

world would be uninhabited. Thus there is no contradiction between Pascal's two modes of understanding. The only possibility is a complementary
relationship between "the omnipresence of consciousness and its involvement in a field of presence."

3 / Phenomenology in the Natural Attitude

IN THIS CHAPTER we will be commenting largely on the Preface to *Phenomenology of Perception* (pp. vii–xxi). The phenomenological approach to the problems of perception and reflection seeks to avoid the antinomies which embroil idealism and realism. "The whole question is ultimately one of understanding what, in ourselves and in the world, is the relation between *significance* and *absence of signification.*" [1] However, the results of a phenomenological critique are not to be gained except as a recovery of meaning from its alienation in philosophical idealism and realism considered as essential moments in the history of the western spirit. There is no phenomenological result apart from the experience through which it comes about, in which it remains essentially open to its own history and the intersubjectivity of interpretation and critique.

1. *Ibid.*, p. 428.

"Phenomenology is accessible only through a phenomenological method." [2] Thus Merleau-Ponty lays upon any commentator the most stringent requirement for the comprehension of a philosophy which is self-consciously the recuperation of the history of philosophy and, therefore, as necessary to what it presupposes as it is impossible without what went before it and seemed always to presage it. To some it may seem that to pose the problem of interpretation in this manner is to intrude unnecessarily the style of Hegelian phenomenology whose dialectical certainties are entirely foreign to Husserl's "unfinished" phenomenology. It would be foolish, indeed, for the sake of a superficial expression, to introduce problems of comparative exegesis which might carry us far from our central theme, which is, as Merleau-Ponty expresses it above, the problem of the relation between meaning, presence and absence. What we have in mind is that in both Hegel and Husserl there is a dialectical relation between a presentification of meaning which is realized before (für) consciousness and the participation of consciousness in this process as its proper intentionality, essential to its full manifestation. That is to say, consciousness in the natural attitude is already an anticipation of consciousness-in-and-for-itself; its forgetfulness of itself is already the path by which it may come to self-recognition. But this means that a phenomenological reduction cannot pretend to suspend the existence or facticity which is presupposed

2. *Ibid.*, p. viii.

by the negativity of consciousness nor can it recover any level prior to language and intersubjectivity as the presupposition of the dialectic of the self-recognition of consciousness.

It is not the intention, nor is it within the competency of this writer, to develop a phenomenology of phenomenology. What is attempted here is to follow a phase in the critical reconstruction of the history of phenomenology to be found in the highly original interpretation and inspiration that results from Merleau-Ponty's relation to Husserlian phenomenology. Such a procedure is justified not so much by the considerable knowledge of Husserliana which Merleau-Ponty possessed, for we are not interested primarily in documentation,[3] but by the light which it

3. The problem of the relation of Merleau-Ponty's thought to his sources calls for a separate essay on his conception of philosophy as interrogation. "Between an 'objective' history of philosophy (which would rob the great philosophers of what they have given others to think about) and a meditation disguised as a dialogue (in which we would ask the questions and give the answers) there must be a middle-ground on which the philosopher we are speaking about and the philosopher who is speaking are present together, although it is not possible even in principle to decide at any given moment just what belongs to each" (*Signs,* trans. Richard C. McCleary [Evanston, Ill.: Northwestern University Press, 1964], p. 159). With this in mind, the documentary study of Merleau-Ponty's reading of Husserl is enormously aided by the essay of H. L. van Breda, "Maurice Merleau-Ponty et les Archives-Husserl à Louvain," *Revue de métaphysique et de morale,* no. 4 (1962), 410–30; and Merleau-Ponty, "Philosophy as Interrogation" and "Husserl at the Limits of Phenomenology," *Themes from the Lectures at the Collège de France, 1952–1960,* trans. John

hopes to throw upon the *motivation* or style of the phenomenological reduction.

In Husserl's own confrontation with the problematic of the phenomenological reduction, Merleau-Ponty discerned a progressive integration of the eidetic and transcendental reductions as negative and positive moments in a reflection which withdraws us from the natural attitude only in order to reveal to us the project towards the world which we are. Thus the motive of the reduction is to restore us in wonder before a world which understands us in the same way that we understand the world.

> All the misunderstandings with his [Husserl's] interpreters, with the existentialist "dissidents" and finally with himself, have arisen from the fact that in order to see the world and grasp it as paradoxical, we must break with our familiar acceptance of it and, also, from the fact that from this break we can learn nothing but the unmotivated upsurge of the world. The most important lesson which the reduction teaches us is the impossibility of a complete reduction.[4]

There would be no motivation for the phenomenological reduction if we were absolute mind. The problem of motivation exists because, on the contrary, we are in the world and the process of reflection is carried out in a temporal flux in which we dwell and in which we perceive that the world is there already latent with our own future. Hence the

O'Neill (Evanston, Ill.: Northwestern University Press, 1970).

4. *Phenomenology of Perception,* p. xiv.

motive for the phenomenological reduction is archaeological, a quest for our origins suspended in wonder at what it always knew was there to be found. There is an inversion at the heart of our teleology: the knowledge of last things awaits us from the very beginning.

In the Preface to *Phenomenology of Perception,* we find Merleau-Ponty raising the question What is Phenomenology? still unanswered fifty years after Husserl's first works. But the lack of a definition and the absence of a phenomenological system is no reproach to phenomenology. Rather is it characteristic of its style as a reflection upon our openness toward the world as a solicitation prior to all categorization and predication. Thus Merleau-Ponty's account of the nature of phenomenology is, so to speak, a report in progress, both in its initial formulation and in the later reconsiderations which supplement it. Phenomenology is a philosophy which embraces antinomies. It is an eidetic analysis. Yet it considers the comprehension of man and the world impossible from any other basis than the facticity of existence. It is a transcendental philosophy which "puts out of play" the existence of the world as we hold to it in the natural attitude. But it does so only to recuperate the correlativity of the world and the intentionalities that bind us to it. Thus it proposes phenomenological descriptions of space, time and the world as "lived experiences," while also professing to be a "rigorous science." And, as though to turn back upon his own starting point,

Husserl in his later works speaks of a "genetic phenomenology," whereas he had professed to describe experience as it is, apart from the causal analysis of the natural and social sciences.

It is striking that Merleau-Ponty gives no prominence to the notion of intentionality in his presentation of phenomenology.[5] Too often considered the principal discovery of phenomenology, the concept of intentionality can in fact only be understood through the reduction. But the "problematic of reduction" is one which never ceased to concern Husserl. For this reason Merleau-Ponty is insistent that any attempt to develop phenomenology which takes the reduction as given is premature.[6] What must absorb our interest is precisely Husserl's emphasis upon the tension between the natural attitude and the results of phenomenological reflection. "C'est l'expérience muette encore qu'il s'agit d'amener à l'expression pure de son propre sens." Such a definition of the task of phenomenology renders it almost impossible. How shall we bring brute experience to yield its meaning? How shall we bring the silence of things into the discourse (la parole) of philosophy?

5. "In our opinion Husserl's originality lies beyond the notion of intentionality: it is to be found in the elaboration of this notion and in the discovery, beneath the intentionality of representations, of a deeper intentionality, which others have called existence" (*ibid.*, p. 121, n. 5).

6. We are paraphrasing Merleau-Ponty's remarks in the discussion which follows the paper by A. de Waelhens, "L'Idée de la phénoménologie," *Husserl*, Cahiers de Royaumont, Philosophie No. III (Paris: Minuit, 1959), pp. 157–69.

Thus understood, phenomenology is founded upon a conflict and tension rather than upon a pre-established harmony.

Every reduction is necessarily both transcendental and eidetic (*Ideen* pp. 59–60). That is to say, we are not able to submit the stream of our perceptions to philosophical reflection without withdrawing from the flux of lived experience and the world which we naturally posit. In philosophical reflection we are obliged to pass from the *fact* of existence (*Dasein*) to the *nature* (*Wesen*) or articulation of the world upon which our existence opens. Thus there can never be any coincidence between reflection and the stream of perception. For it is precisely the task of reflection to disengage things and the world from the perception of the world by subjecting them to a systematic variation that reveals "intelligible clusters" which nevertheless retain an impenetrable aspect. Thus, from the very fact that every reduction is initially eidetic, it follows that it can never yield an adequation of thought and experience, since there always remains a separation between experience and the eidos, a separation required, indeed, by philosophical reflection. It may even be questioned whether it is ever possible to adopt the standpoint of pure transcendental consciousness. For we cannot avoid reflection upon the source of the resistance which lived experience offers to reflection. It is not enough simply to acknowledge this resistance as a nameless adversity. It is an experience outside of the experience of tran-

scendental consciousness which has its own truth
and value, of which we must provide an account.

The sense which Merleau-Ponty drew from these
difficulties in the reduction lies in the direction of
what we have decided to describe as a phenomenology in the natural attitude. By this we mean a phenomenology in which the reduction is employed as a
means rather than an end in order to reveal within
the facticity of our existence a proto-genesis of the
world and reflection. "Husserl's essences are des-
tined to bring back all the living relationships of
experience, as the fisherman's net draws up from
the depths of the ocean quivering fish and sea-
weed." [7] Merleau-Ponty's conception of phenomenology is rooted in a philosophy of life and nature which he was still working on in *The Visible
and the Invisible* [8] when he died.

The phenomenological method, guided by Husserl's prescription of a return to the "things themselves," is a method of description which excludes
equally the procedures of scientific explanation and
analytical reflection. "To return to things themselves is to return to that world which precedes
knowledge, of which knowledge always *speaks*, and
in relation to which every scientific schematization
is an abstract and derivative sign-language as is
geography in relation to the countryside in which we
have learnt beforehand what a forest, a prairie or a

7. *Phenomenology of Perception,* p. xv.
8. *The Visible and the Invisible,* followed by Working
Notes, ed. Claude Lefort, trans. Alphonso Lingis (Evanston,
Ill.: Northwestern University Press, 1968).

river is." [9] At the same time, this move is not a
retreat into the unsituated remoteness of a consciousness which lays down the laws of experience
while enjoying its own immunity. Phenomenological reflection is not a retreat from the world toward
a basis in the transcendental unity of consciousness;
it separates the intentional lines between us and the
world in order to uncover the umbilical cord that ties
us to the world.

> Husserl's transcendental is not Kant's and Husserl
> accuses Kant's philosophy of being "worldly," because
> it *makes use* of our relation to the world, which is the
> motive force of the transcendental deduction, and
> makes the world immanent in the subject, instead of
> *being filled with wonder* at it and conceiving the sub-
> ject as a process of transcendence towards the world. [10]

Nevertheless, for a very long time Husserl's
presentation of the reduction remains in terms of a
return to a transcendental consciousness before
which the world is a transparent term. We shall
have to take up the critical developments involved
here. Their consideration will serve us as the transition to the second phase of Merleau-Ponty's interpretation of Husserl's turning toward a phenomenology in the natural attitude.

We consider now an example of what Merleau-
Ponty regarded as a genuine phenomenological reduction involved in the critique of the constancy
hypothesis. In the language of the psychology of

9. *Ibid.*, p. ix.
10. *Ibid.*, p. xiv.

perception we find the notions of sensation and attention which are not confirmed by the experience of perception but are introduced as hypotheses in favor of the prejudice of an objective, determinate world. Red is not a sensation or an element of consciousness, but a property of the object, a red cheek or a red sky, and has a meaning that only becomes determinate in the lived world, in what mothers perceive, or shepherds.

> There are two ways of being mistaken about quality: one is to make it into an element of consciousness, when in fact it is an object *for* consciousness, to treat it as an incommunicable impression, whereas it always has a meaning; the other is to think that this meaning and this object, at the level of quality, are fully developed and determinate. The second error, like the first, springs from our prejudice about the world.[11]

For example, the two straight lines in Muller-Lyer's optical illusion are neither of equal nor unequal length.

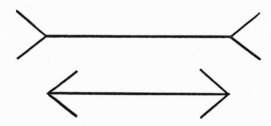

11. *Ibid.*, p. 5.

This is a problem which belongs in the construction of an objective world which can tell us nothing about the *field of vision*. In the visual field we do not see the two lines in a realm which permits comparison; we experience the lines as each having its own universe. To introduce the notion of attention in order to save the "analytic perception" of the two main lines in the figure as the case of "normal perception" is merely to presuppose rather than to establish the constancy hypothesis. The analytic method forces the phenomenal universe into categories which only make sense in the discourse of science. In the objective "reality" of science two equal lines should always appear equal in perception—indeed, this constitutes the "normal case." What in fact occurs for perception in Muller-Lyer's illusion is that one of the lines ceases to be equal to the other without thereby becoming "unequal": it becomes "different." By its nature, perception naturally admits the ambiguous and the shifting and is shaped by its context. For perception, an isolated line and the same line taken in a figure cease to be the "same" line, and it is only "second nature" to perceive the lines as identical. "The theory of sensation, which builds up all knowledge out of determinate qualities, offers us objects purged of all ambiguity, pure and absolute, the ideal rather than the real themes of knowledge: in short, it is compatible only with the lately developed superstructure of consciousness." [12]

12. *Ibid.*, p. 11.

The theory of sensation admits only a nominalist account of meaning through contiguity and association. Formalism, instead of explaining the structure of perception in terms of association, attempts to reconstruct it through the notion of "judgment" as *what sensation lacks to make perception possible*. Perception is reduced to an interpretation of signs furnished through the senses in accordance with physiological stimuli. But since the least sensible phenomenon involves an excess over the physical impression, every sense experience involves judgment and we lose sight of the function of judgment as the constitution of truth, without getting any closer to the experience of meaning in the sensible prior to all prediction. If every perception involves judgment, then we cannot distinguish true and false judgments formally but are obliged to have recourse to a purely conjectural layer of objective impressions to be translated, correctly or incorrectly, in the operation of judgment. But, of course, it is precisely the original compossibility of veridical and illusory perception that remains to be explained. Authentic reflection must explain how there comes to be a meaning in the sensible figure; it must describe the perceptual syntax which is the matrix of truth and illusion.

> Empiricism cannot see that we need to know what we are looking for, otherwise we would not be looking for it, and intellectualism fails to see that we need to be ignorant of what we are looking for, or equally again we should not be searching. They are in agree-

ment in that neither attaches due importance to that circumscribed ignorance, that still "empty" but already determinate intention which *is* attention itself.[13]

It is through our incarnation that we operate a correlation of perception and the world, a circumscription of ignorance in the terrain between silence and lucidity that implies a new theory of natural reflection and a *tacit cogito*. We know that at first children distinguish colored objects only in a general way from colorless objects. Thereafter, colored objects are further distinguished in terms of "warm" and "cold" colors, and finally detailed color discriminations are acquired. The empiricist prejudice of determinacy requires that we say the child sees a color *where it is* but has not yet learned to associate a name with it, rather than recognize that color discrimination is a secondary formation which presupposes an original acquisition of the color-quality as a structure of consciousness. The first act of perception is to acquire for itself a *field* in which the movements of the exploratory organ become possible. The moon when seen through a cardboard tube looks no bigger on the horizon than at the zenith. But we have no reason to believe that the sixpenny moon is the one we see on the horizon unaided by instruments whose results reflect nothing more than the principles of their own construction. "When I look quite freely and naturally, the various parts of the field interact and *motivate* this enormous moon

13. *Ibid.*, p. 28.

on the horizon, this measureless size which nevertheless is a size." [14] Similarly, there is no reason to ignore the role of our marginal perception of the intervening objects between us and an object in the distance upon which we fix our eye. For when these intervening objects are screened there appears a shrinkage in the apparent distance and when we remove the screen we see distance generated, as it were, by the intervening objects. "This is the silent language whereby perception communicates with us: interposed objects, in the natural context, 'mean' a greater distance. It is not, however, a question of a connection recognized by objective logic, the logic of constituted truth: for there is *no reason* why a steeple should appear to me to be smaller and farther away when I am better able to see in detail the slopes and fields between me and it. There is no reason, but there is a *motive*." [15] The mode of existence which objects come to have for perceptual consciousness requires a mode of description other than causal analysis and reconstruction.

On the other hand, the phenomenological notion of *motivation* is one of those "fluid" concepts which have to be formed if we want to get back to phenomena. One phenomenon releases another, not by means of some objective cause, like those which link together natural events, but by the meaning which it holds out—there is an underlying reason for a thing which

14. *Ibid.*, p. 31.
15. *Ibid.*, p. 48, emphasis on "motive" added.

guides the flow of phenomena without being explicitly laid down in any of them, *a sort of operative reason.*[16]

There is a natural perception, a non-thetic mode of consciousness which is not yet in possession of fully determinate objects or of any explicit logic, but which is nevertheless conformed to the style of the world as its own immanent logic. It was in order to get at this level of proto-reflection that it was necessary to subject the concepts of empiricist and formal psychology to a phenomenological reduction. We see that the attempt of classical psychology to reconstruct veridical perception involves a secondary reconstruction which remains in the natural attitude, for the reason that it still presupposes the *originating* experience of perception as the appropriation of *significations* which are the condition of the values assumed by determinate perceptions. We need to distinguish the notions of structure and significance.[17] The Gestalt or structure of the circle is engendered according to a rule of understanding. The significance of a circle is its physiognomy as a modulation of consciousness and its world. The former is constructed in accordance with a norm, the latter is *a birth of a norm*, the conformation of the external and the internal and not the projection of the internal upon the external.

What makes phenomenology a phenomenology is that it is not confined to seeking the conditions of the possibility of being but is a genealogy of being,

16. *Ibid.*, pp. 49–50, final emphasis added.
17. *The Structure of Behavior*, pp. 145–60.

that is, "a study of the *advent* of being into consciousness, instead of presuming its possibility given in advance." [18] We see now that what distinguishes the phenomenological concept of intentionality from the Kantian relation to a possible object is that the unity of the phenomenal world is experienced as already there for the incarnate subject whose nature is spontaneously conformed to the world as its behavioral field.

It is a question of recognizing consciousness itself as a project of the world, meant for the world which it neither embraces nor possesses, but towards which it is perpetually directed—and the world as this preobjective individual whose imperious unity decrees what knowledge shall take as its goal. This is why Husserl distinguishes between *intentionality of act,* which is that of our judgments and of those occasions when we voluntarily take up a position—the only intentionality discussed in the *Critique of Pure Reason* —and *operative intentionality (fungierende Intentionalität),* or that which produces the natural and antepredicative unity of the world and our life, being apparent in our desires, our evaluations and in the landscape we see, more clearly than in objective knowledge, and furnishing the text which our knowledge tries to translate into precise language. Our relationship to the world, as it is untiringly enunciated within us, is not a thing which can be any further clarified by analysis; philosophy can only place it once more before our eyes and present it for our ratification. [19]

18. *Phenomenology of Perception,* p. 61.
19. *Ibid.,* p. xvii, emphasis added.

4 / Corporeality
   and Intersubjectivity

IN THIS SECTION WE CONTINUE our commentary on the basis of the essay "Le Philosophe et son ombre." [1] It is a characteristic of the progression of Merleau-Ponty's thought that his conclusions represent fresh starting-points. Thus the concluding evaluation of the contribution of phenomenology is beset with new problems which we need to take up in a second-order reflection upon the phenomenon of the phenomenon. "Probably the chief gain from phenomenology is to have united extreme subjectivism and extreme objectivism in its notion of the world or rationality. . . . To say that there exists rationality is to say that perspectives blend, percep-

1. First published in *Edmund Husserl, 1859–1959, Receuil commémoratif publié à l'occasion du centenaire de la naissance du philosophe, Phaenomenologica* IV (The Hague: Martinus Nijhoff, 1959), pp. 195–220; reprinted in *Signes,* (Paris: Gallimard, 1960), pp. 201–29 (*Signs,* pp. 159–81).

tions confirm each other, a meaning emerges." [2] The world is never given to us as a flat surface over which we cast our speculative glance. Our world is given to us in the hollows between things, as the field of our exploratory senses which polarize objects as the immanent ends of our intentions, in the paths where the experience of others and ourselves intersect and blend together. "Rationality is not a *problem.*" Our everyday experience witnesses to the network of relationships between us and things and between ourselves and other people that we literally are as incarnate subjects. We may say that, though not a problem, rationality or the phenomenon of a common world is a mystery; but it is a mystery solved through our corporeality which is our intersubjectivity no less than our subjectivity.

Nevertheless, phenomenology experiences temptations in the course of bringing its precious cargo to port, and to reach home it must hug the contours of the land rather than sail by the stars. For a long time phenomenology remains obsessed by a transcendental unity which is the impartial law of the spectacle of the world in myself and others. The transcendental ego is the norm which makes possible a common world but remains blind to its own ontogenesis, the contingency of its inherence in a particular subject who never has more than a partial comprehension of a world not of his making. Nor can there be any recognition of the problem of intersubjectivity where Peter and Paul exist solely

2. *Phenomenology of Perception,* p. xix.

as values of a consciousness which confronts the world as its immanent universal. Phenomenology recognizes that the *alter ego* is a paradox. While the *cogito* defines *me* as the thought which I have of myself, and which I am alone in having, then it is never I that the other sees when he sees me, unless I am the exterior which I present to others.

> For the "other" to be more than an empty word, it is necessary that my existence should never be reduced to my bare awareness of existing, but that it should take in also the awareness that *one* may have of it, and thus include my incarnation in some nature and the possibility, at least, of a historical situation. The *Cogito* must reveal me in a situation, and it is on this condition alone that transcendental subjectivity can, as Husserl puts it, *be* an intersubjectivity.[3]

The final condition of phenomenology is a "return" to a philosophy of nature,[4] always present in Husserl's troubled reflection upon the phenomenological reduction, and the unbroken circle of Merleau-Ponty's own thought from the *Structure of Behavior* to *The Visible and the Invisible*. In *Ideen* I, § 50, there is a progression in which the intentional relation between consciousness and nature is transformed into the contingency of nature relative to absolute consciousness which emerges from the natural attitude by operating (*vollziehen*), ideally, a suspension of any empirical order given to it. Thus

3. *Ibid.*, pp. xii–xiii.
4. "Husserl et la notion de nature, notes prises au cours de Maurice Merleau-Ponty," *Revue de métaphysique et de morale*, no. 3 (1965), 257–69.

the reduction of the natural attitude merges with
the transcendental constitution. Nevertheless, Merleau-Ponty argues that the direction of phenomenology, by the time of *Ideen* II, is not that of the
philosophy of mind.[5] The distinction between a pure
subject and pure things (*blosse Sachen*), the disin-
terested knower who grasps things simply as things,
is rendered problematic in the search for a more
fundamental relation to being which relativizes the
"theoretical attitude." The transcendence of the natural world is not simply the antithesis of its transcendental immanence in "reduced" consciousness.
The ontological milieu which our natural life intends is not a theoretical attitude, far less is it a
natural "attitude," which we might refuse to enter-
tain.[6]

5. "Husserl in his last period concedes that all reflection
should in the first place return to the description of the
world of living experience (*Lebenswelt*). But he adds that,
by means of a second 'reduction,' the structures of the world
of experience must be reinstated in the transcendental flow
of a universal constitution in which all the world's obscuri-
ties are elucidated. It is clear, however, that we are faced
with a dilemma: either the constitution makes the world
transparent, in which case it is not obvious why reflection
needs to pass through the world of experience, or else it re-
tains something of that world, and never rids it of its opacity. Husserl's thought moves increasingly in this second direction, despite many throwbacks to the logicist period—as
is seen when he makes a problem of rationality, when he
allows significances which are in the last resort 'fluid'
(*Erfahrung und Urteil*, p. 482), when he bases knowledge
on a basic δoξa" (*Phenomenology of Perception*, p. 365, n. 1).
6. "If that is what it is, it relapses into the Cartesian
error of the *hypothesis of a Nichtigkeit of the world*, whose
immediate consequence is the postulation of an indubitable
mens sive anima (part of the world)——Every negation of

But this is what is maintained in the view of mind and nature held by the philosophical reflection which underlies scientific *naturalism*.

> The natural attitude really becomes an attitude—a tissue of judicatory and propositional acts—only when it becomes a naturalist thesis. The natural attitude itself emerges unscathed from the complaints which can be made about naturalism, because it is "prior to all thesis," because it is the mystery of a *Weltthesis* prior to all theses. It is, Husserl says in another connection, the mystery of a primordial faith and a fundamental and original opinion (*Urglaube, Urdoxa*) which are thus not even in principle translatable in terms of clear and distinct knowledge, and which—more ancient than any "attitude" or

---

the world, *but equally* any neutrality with regard to the existence of the world, has the immediate consequence that it loses hold of the transcendental. The *epoché* is properly a neutral attitude only in regard to the world as effectively closed upon itself, as pure externality: it must allow the subsistence of this self-contained phenomenon, this externality.

"The transcendental field is a field of transcendencies. Inasmuch as it is the resolute surpassing of a *mens sive natura* and the realm of psychology, the transcendental is the transcendence of subjectivity in the sense of counter-transcendence and immanence. Husserl is right to remark that the transition to intersubjectivity is only contradictory in an incomplete reduction. A complete reduction, on the other hand, leads beyond the pretended transcendental 'immanence'; it leads to the absolute spirit, understood as *Weltlichkeit,* to the *Geist* as an *Ineinander* of spontaneities, itself grounded upon an aesthesiological *Ineinander* and on the sphere of life as a sphere of Einfühlung and intercorporality——The notion of the *species* = notion of interanimality. The interweaving of biology or psychology and philosophy = *Selbstheit* of the *world*" (*The Visible and the Invisible,* pp. 171–72, modified).

"point of view"—give us not a representation of the world but the world itself.[7]

The relationship between the transcendental and natural attitudes is better described as circular rather than sequential or parallel. *There is a preparation for phenomenology in the natural attitude,* a "pretheoretical constitution" which is natural to incarnate consciousness. At the same time, the transcendental attitude poses itself as a question for itself, in an infinite mediation upon the relation between reflection and that which resists reflection . . .

and the ultimate task of phenomenology as philosophy of consciousness is to understand its relationship to non-phenomenology. What resists phenomenology within us—natural being, the "barbarous" source Schelling spoke of—cannot remain outside of phenomenology and should have its place within it. The philosopher bears with him his shadow which is not simply the material absence of light from the future.[8]

The philosopher is not a disembodied consciousness contemplating objects which exist only in the light of mind. The philosopher is an embodied consciousness open to objects through the same light and shadow cast by his own body. The world is given to us primordially not in the *cogito,* but in the incarnate subject (*Subjektleib*) as a *Possum* (I am able to). It is through the body that we discover a "subject-ob-

7. *Signs*, p. 163.
8. *Ibid.*, p. 178; the concluding phrase is my translation.

ject" relationship which is the definitive articulation of an "irrelative" in perceptual experience that is the "statutory basis" (*Rechtsgrund*) of all the constructions of the understanding. Through my body I experience a spiritualization of matter and a materialization of spirit, the enigma of sensible matter given to itself through a "sort of reflection" (*eine Art von Reflexion*). When I touch my right hand with my left I experience the right hand as a physical thing which almost simultaneously begins to reverse the process, *es wird Leib, es empfindet* (*Ideen* II, 145). Here we can no longer understand intentionality as the "idea" of the coincidence of the subject and object; intentionality lies in the *reversibility* of the objective and phenomenal body, that is, in the "flesh of the world." My body is the zero point at which there opens up a world and others, separated from me by an *aesthetic distance* which I am sure of crossing with a glance, but which I can never totally embrace.[9]

9. "To touch and to touch oneself (to touch oneself = the touching-touched) cannot coincide in the body: what touches is never quite what is touched. That does not mean that they coincide "in the mind," or at the level of "consciousness." Something more than the body is needed to bring about this conjuncture: it occurs in the *untouchable* ——that which in the other I can never touch. But what I can never touch, he, too, cannot touch. So there is no privilege of oneself over the other in this case, and therefore it is not consciousness which is the untouchable—— "Consciousness" would have to be something positive, and so it would or does recreate the duality of the reflecting–reflected upon in terms of that of the touching-touched. The untouchable is not something touchable which happens to be inaccessible——the unconscious is not a representation in

Nevertheless there remains a problem of *solipsism*. The generality of the body remains the other side of an inalienable consciousness present to itself even in the act of self-sacrifice. How are we to find *elsewhere* in the perceptual field such a presence of self to self. The problem of intersubjectivity is here identical with the problem of transcendental subjectivity in general, namely, *"how the presence to myself* (Urpräsenz) *which establishes my own limits and conditions every alien presence is at the same time depresentation* (Entgegenwärtigung) *and throws me outside myself."* [10] And in this case reflection must as in all other cases reveal something of its object in an unreflective experience of the other, or we should not be able to present to ourselves the problem of solipsism. It is in the tissue of sensible being that the other person is given to me as I am given to myself—the prereflexive *cogito* is not a struggle to the death but a coexistence of consciousnesses. Thus when I shake another person's hand there occurs a similar reversibility of the touching-touched—I experience a different sensibility (*Emp-*

------

practice inaccessible. The negative in this case is not a *positive which is elsewhere* (a transcendent)——It is a real negative, that is, an *Unverborgenheit* of the *Verborgenheit,* an *Urpräsentation* of the *Nichturpräsentierbar.* In other words, it is the originary source of the *elsewhere,* a *Selbst* which is an Other, a Fold——Therefore there is no sense at all in saying that the junction between the touching-touched is effected by Thought or Consciousness: Thought or Consciousness is *Offenheit* of a corporeity to . . . World or Being" (*The Visible and the Invisible,* p. 254, modified).

10. *Phenomenology of Perception,* p. 363.

findbarkeit), another perceiving body prior to the secondary constructions of soul and personality. Nor is this a process of *introjection*. It is not simply an "I think *that* he thinks" in which the *cogito* would still fail to escape from itself.

> Man can create the alter ego which "thought" cannot create, because he is outside himself in the world and because one ekstasis is compossible with other ekstases. And that possibility is fulfilled in perception as vinculum of brute being and a body. The whole riddle of *Einfühlung* lies in its initial, "esthesiological" phase; and it is solved there because it is a perception. He who "posits" the other man is a perceiving subject, the other person's body is a perceived thing, and the other person himself is "posited" as "perceiving." It is never a matter of anything but co-perception. I see that this man over there sees, as I touch my left hand while it is touching my right.[11]

Thus we see that we are no longer forced to develop the phenomenological reduction and its existential condition or facticity as alternatives; for the intentional correlative of the world is not the transcendental Ego but intersubjectivity. The Husserlian reflection is both an analytics of essences and an analytics of existences. Husserl's conception of Nature is one of a world of objects fundamentally present to sensible being and ideally to a community of sensible beings. There is no longer any question of a direct ontology or constitution, but only of an incomplete reduction which reveals the *Weltthesis*.

11. *Signs*, p. 170.

"La Nature est cette chance offerte à la corporeité et à l'intersubjectivité." But this is only possible because our corporeality possesses a power of self-forgetfulness (*Selbstvergessenheit*) [12] which is the source of the transition from the latent to the theoretical constitution, which in turn is only a test of our primordial bond with the world and others. Originally an attempt to conquer the world as the mind's creature, the constitution becomes the revelation of the world as the earth and native abode of rationality. The facticity of the world and our incarnation is the lesson of patience; and the phenomenological description is ultimately a meditation "as painstaking as the works of Balzac, Proust, Valéry or Cézanne—by reason of the same kind of attentiveness and wonder, the same demand for awareness, the same will to seize the emergent meaning of the world and of history." [13]

12. "But although it is of the essence of consciousness to forget its own phenomena thus enabling 'things' to be constituted, this forgetfulness is not a mere absence, it is the absence of something which consciousness could bring into its presence: in other words consciousness can forget phenomena only because it can recall them, it neglects them only because they are the cradle of things" (*Phenomenology of Perception*, p. 59).

13. *Ibid.*, p. xxi, modified.

5 / Institution, Language, and Historicity

WE MAY NOW BE IN A POSITION to interpret Merleau-Ponty's suggestion that we conceive consciousness as institution rather than constitution.[1] We need to understand how consciousness is given to itself neither all at once nor at the expense of others but in a field of presence and coexistence which situates consciousness and truth as a sedimentation and a search. The notion of consciousness as institution restores subjectivity and objectivity to the matrix in which conduct is generated as a recovery of being which is simultaneously self discovery.

Thus what we understand by the concept of institution are those events in an experience which endow

1. "Institution in Personal and Public History," in *Themes from the Lectures at the Collège de France, 1952–1960*, trans. John O'Neill (Evanston, Ill.: Northwestern University Press, 1970).

it with dimensions durable, in relation to which a whole series of other experiences will acquire meaning, will form an intelligible series or a history—or again the events which sediment in me a meaning not just as survivals or residues, but as the invitation to a sequel, the necessity of a future.[2]

The temporal ekstasis of the instituting consciousness is the acquisition and renovation of a style of being through its openness to expression and conduct. This is to say that consciousness is never a real adequation of the self to itself, but rather an intentional unity whose infrastructure is temporality or historicity precisely because it is only in subjectivity that there is found that possibility of not-being which delineates past and future, whereas the plenum is too solidary for there to be temporality.[3]

The significance of time comes from what we are and what objects can be for us. Subject and object are, in other words, "two abstract 'moments' of a unique structure which is presence." It is in the field of presence that there is consciousness of what has passed and what is to come; and this field lies in the hollow of the for-itself, the revelation of the self to the self. We are present to a world which is carried forward along vectors of intentionality which trace out the style of the world to come. The present, in the strict sense of a "now," is not posited by us. "I do not so much perceive objects as reckon with an environment; I seek support in my tools,

2. *Ibid.*, pp. 40–41.
3. *Phenomenology of Perception*, p. 412.

and I am at my task rather than confronting it." The present is the privileged zone in which being and consciousness coincide, not in the sense that our being is reducible to the knowledge we have of it—for perception reveals only our primitive alliance with the world—but in the sense that consciousness is nothing but belonging to the world and thereby to ourselves as ecstatic beings. The discovery of the self is not an a-temporal act, but rather, we must think of subjectivity as temporality, the search for a meaning that can never be absolutely totalized. It is not, of course, that our gestures and thoughts never succeed in expressing our intentions, nor that it is impossible to detect meaning in historical events. It is rather that in the creative act or expression there is no meaning which precedes it and which it simply translates. Its meaning is discovered in the act of expression as the style of the world revealed through the vehicle of the artist, the statesman or the speaking subject, all of whom discover their own meaning as a correlative of the expressive gesture.

The institution of self-consciousness no less than the institution of ideas, truth and culture, is founded upon a series of exchanges between subjectivity and situation in which the polarities of means and ends and question and answer are continuously established and renewed. The model of such exchanges is to be found in the relation of consciousness to language and speech and may also serve as an introduction to other cultural institutions, including history and the social sciences themselves as symbolic institutions. This suggestion is the result of abandoning the attempt to construct an eidetic of all possible symbolic structures as the correlative of a universal and timeless constituting consciousness as first conceived by Husserl and which raised its own difficulties with regard to intersubjectivity, rationality and philosophy itself.[4]

Starting from the later writings of Husserl and from Saussure's work in linguistics,[5] a conception of the relation of language to consciousness emerges in which, so far from being an external instrument of thought, language appears as the embodiment of thought without which thought would achieve neither ideal existence nor intersubjective value. Language is not simply a mnemonic device that thought employs in order to facilitate its expression but might discard for wings of its own. We express our thought by bringing it to inhabit the spoken word (*la parole*): we know what we have in mind (*vouloir dire*) or what we mean once we know how to say it, by a kind of permutation of the intentional object and its embodiment in an expressive gesture. The incarnation of thought in the word (*la parole,*

4. "On the Phenomenology of Language," in *Signs*, p. 85.
5. Merleau-Ponty's interpretation of Saussure must first of all be understood in terms of his reading of Husserl which determines his interest in the ontogenesis of speech, and his interpolation of a psychology lacking in Saussure but complementary to the line of development that Merleau-Ponty introduces. Cf. "The Problem of Speech," in *Themes from the Lectures at the Collège de France*, pp. 19–26; and Maurice Lageux, "Merleau-Ponty et la linguistique de Saussure," *Dialogue*, IV, no. 3 (1965), 351–64.

logos) actualizes the transcendental affinities of thought and being in a process of the recovery of a truth which can never be absolutely totalized.

> It is like a wedge that we sink into the present, a landmark which testifies that at this moment something has happened for which being was always waiting or intending to say from the very beginning, and which will never cease, if not to be true, at least to be significant and to arouse our thinking resources to the need for drawing from it truths more comprehensive than itself.[6]

Since perception never reveals to us a totality and our perspectives fall upon a world which encloses them, our expression of the world in language, thought and art can never be the prose reproduction of a pre-established nature. We express the world through the poetics of our own being-in-the-world, beginning with the first act of perception which carves into being the perspectives of form and ground whereby the world has an architecture or foundation. In the gesture of pointing our body opens up a world whose schema it bears within itself and through which it possesses the world, as it were, at a distance. All other cultural gestures are continuous with the first gesture of human behavior in opening up a world which expresses meaning by an indirection that takes root in us as the fruit of human labor and is never a completed task.

The ontological bearing of language may be clarified if we draw a distinction between *language* as

6. *Signs*, p. 96.

an objective structure studied by linguistics and *speech* which is the use-value language acquires when it is turned toward expression. It is not because they are the sign-correlates of mental significations that words succeed in conveying thought. Rather than interpose themselves between us and what we mean to say, words signify only through the texture of our discourse which at any given moment is nothing more than a *"determinate gap* to be filled in by words." [7] Our "thoughts" find expression through a sensible articulation of which we are capable without prior reflection because we are, as Valéry says, the "animal of words." [8] In speech there occurs a reversal of language which has us and language which we make ours through a series of "coherent deformations" (Malraux) which anchor new meaning for ourselves and our listeners. The manner in which this is achieved involves an institution of meaning in which both speaker and listener, writer and reader, share in the same expressive operation of the recuperation and innovation of a style of language. We start by reading an author, leaning at first upon the common associations of his words until, gradually, they begin to flow in us and to open us to an original sound which is the writer's voice borrowing from us an understanding which until then we did not know was ours to offer. "I say

7. *Ibid.*, p. 89.
8. "Studies in the Literary Usage of Language," in *Themes from the Lectures at the Collège de France*, pp. 12–18.

that I *know an idea* when the capacity to organize
around it discourses which make sense has been
instituted in me; and this capacity itself does not
depend upon my alleged possession and face to face
contemplation of it, but upon my having acquired a
certain style of thinking." [9] Once we have acquired
the author's style of thinking, our lives interweave
in a presence which is the anticipation (*Vorhaben*)
in the words of the whole of the author's intention
and its simultaneous recovery (*Nachvollzug*) which
continues the understanding. "A personal and interpersonal tradition will have been founded." [10]

We always mean to say something. That is the
original promise conveyed in the human gaze, gesture, and language, and solicited by the world itself.
The task of expression is simultaneously a self-
improvisation in which we borrow from the world,
others and our own past efforts. The act of expression is not a solitary exercise in initiation, but the
acquisition of a tradition which is the ability to
recover an interrogation opened in the past and to
inscribe it in a living style of expression which it
always called for in its truth. Each act of expression
remains an exemplary type, inaugurates a world
and outlines a future which is not the simple sacri-
fice of the past, but the sedimentation of all presents
in our own—

and just as our body, insofar as it *lives* and makes
itself gesture, sustains itself only through its effort

9. *Signs*, p. 91.
10. *Ibid.*, p. 92.

to be in the world, holds itself upright because its inclination is towards the top and because its perceptual fields draw it toward that risky position, and could not possibly receive this power from a separate spirit; so that history of painting, which runs from one work to another, rests upon itself and is borne only by the caryatid of our efforts, which converge by the sole fact that they are efforts to express.[11]

The object of the historical and social sciences is, properly speaking, neither an object nor an act of contemplation but a verification (*reprise*) which each individual undertakes according to his situation in an attempt, which must be continually reviewed, to unearth sedimented structures of meaning—in a language or a culture. These structures, however, can never be fully brought to life for the reason that they are buried in our own primordial archaeology as an "operant or latent intentionality like that which is the soul of time, more ancient than the intentionality of human acts." [12] A social anthropology which is founded upon a phenomenological description of perceptual consciousness is simultaneously a metaphysical consciousness grounded in the paradox that the life of the individual is also a universal life, not as a biological or species identity but in the community of perception, dialogue and tradition. The appeal of a cultural object, such as a painting, which makes it possible to speak of a universal Art, or history of art, can only

11. "Indirect Language and the Voices of Silence," in *ibid.*, p. 69.
12. "The Philosopher and his Shadow," in *ibid.*, p. 165.

be grasped if we recognize *"un ordre original de l'avènement,"* which is the nature of human expression to inaugurate a value supervenient to the level of fact and open to all other modes of expression insofar as they are similar designations of an order of significance which is continuous from the first gesture to the wall-paintings.

Thus if we were to model history after art and language we might recover the true sense of the concept of history as expression, truth and inter-subjectivity.

> The linguistic relations among men should help us understand the more general order of symbolic relations and of institutions, which assure the exchange not only of thoughts, but of all types of values, the coexistence of men within a culture and, beyond it, within a single history. Interpreted in terms of symbolism . . . history is no more external to us than language.[13]

We should have to distinguish two sorts of historicity which have their origin in the two conceptions of consciousness as constitution and consciousness as institution. Constituting consciousness contemplates the history of art in the dead synthesis of the museum whose rooms present any style of art from an external perspective totally alien to the actual genesis of that style. The other historicity which is presupposed by the museum lies in the artist's institution of his own style from one work to another guided by the same fundamental problem of the

13. *The Primacy of Perception*, p. 9.

world to be painted or described which outlines the history of art and the *interest* the artist has in always starting again. The museum ossifies this living historicity of a work in process into a series of dead-end works of art which reveal nothing of the matrix of acquisition and search in which the artist cannot say what comes from himself, what from others nor what is added or taken away from the question which demanded his response.

Merleau-Ponty remarks how well Husserl's term *Stiftung,* foundation or establishment, captures the fecundity of cultural creations by which they endure into our present and open a field of inquiry to which they are continuously relevant. "It is thus that the world as soon as he has seen it, his first attempts at painting, and the whole past of painting all deliver up a *tradition* to the painter—*that is,* Husserl remarks, *the power to forget origins* and to give to the past not a survival, which is the hypocritical form of forgetfulness, but a new life, which is the noble form of memory." [14] It is the same fecundity which explains the unity of Geometry as an intentional history or intellectual tradition.[15] The ideal unity of Geometry and its historical development derive

14. *Signs,* p. 59.
15. "Husserl at the Limits of Phenomenology," in *Themes from the Lectures at the Collège de France,* pp. 113–22. Merleau-Ponty's interpretation of the relation of constituting consciousness to the medium of language is disputed in Jacques Derrida's masterful introduction and translation of Edmund Husserl's *L'Origine de la géometrie* (Paris: Presses Universitaires de France, 1962), cf. pp. 71 ff. and 122 ff.

from the same source in individual acts of production and reproduction in which the historicity *of* Geometry is as essential to its *history* (*Geschichte*) as is the linguistic tradition which individual geometricians inherit and through which they contribute to the infinite ideal of pure Geometry. Through language and writing what was only an ideal meaning in the mind of an individual achieves an objective and public status, enters a community of thinkers which is the presupposition of truth. Thus we have another instance of that circuit of reflection in which what was first recognized as neither local nor temporal "according to the meaning of its being," comes to rest upon the locality and temporality of speech which belongs neither to the objective world nor the world of ideas.

> Ideal existence is based upon the document, not, of course, as a physical object, or even as the vehicle of one-to-one significations assigned to it by the language in which it is written, but upon the document insofar as, again by an "intentional transgression," it solicits and brings together all lives in pursuit of knowledge—and as such establishes and re-establishes a "Logos" of the cultural world.[16]

What emerges from these examples is that the universality and truth aimed at by theoretical consciousness is not an intrinsic property of the idea. It is an acquisition continuously established and re-established in a community and tradition of science

16. *Signs,* pp. 96–97.

called for and responded to by individuals in specific historical situations. Understood in this way, history is the call of one thought to another, because each individual's work or action is created across the path of self and others towards a *public* which it elicits rather than serves.[17] That is to say, history is the field which individual effort requires in order to become one with the community it seeks to build so that where it is successful its invention appears always to have been necessary. Individual action then is the invention of history because it is shaped in a present which previously was not just a void waiting to be determined by the word or deed, but a tissue of calling and response which is the life of no one and everyone. Every one of life's actions, insofar as it invokes its truth, lives in the expectation of an historical inscription, a judgment not of its intention or consequences but of its fecundity, which is the relevance of its "story" to the present.

> True history thus gets its life entirely from us. It is in our present that it gets the force to refer everything else to the present. The other whom I respect gets his life from me as I get mine from him. A philosophy of history does not take away any of my rights or initiatives. It simply adds to my obligations as a solitary person the obligation to understand situations other than my own and to create a path between my life and that of others, that is, to express myself.[18]

17. "Materials for a Theory of History," in *Themes from the Lectures at the Collège de France*, pp. 27–38.
18. *Signs*, p. 75.

The phenomenology of language and speech yields a basic intuition which liberates history from the false alternatives of materialism and idealism. The institution of language, which makes man and all other institutions possible, proceeds through an ever-open series of exchanges between the assumption of past linguistic acquisitions and the advent of expression which encounters the indirection of the world. In the act of speech the individual achieves an autonomy, an authentic style which at the same time is the declaration of his membership in a continuing linguistic community whose traditions are sedimented in his natural being. This presence of the individual in the institution and of the institution in the individual is particularly clear in the case of linguistic innovations. The need to speak and to be understood leads to new inflections and discriminations in which living speech rearticulates the possibilities of language and finds its innovations incorporated in the sense and history of its language.

Language provides us with more than an analogy for the understanding of the processes of structure and genesis in other social institutions.[19] Just as a language is a system of signs whose values are interdependent or diacritical, so every institution is a symbolic system in which the individual incorpo-

19. "We have here a rationality in contingency, a livid logic, an autoconstitution which is precisely what we need to understand the union of contingency and meaning in history, and Saussure may well have outlined a new philosophy of history" (*Éloge de la philosophie et autres essais* [Paris: Gallimard, 1960], p. 64).

rates himself and through which his actions acquire a typical style. The reciprocal relation between the means of expression and the desire for expression is matched by the institutional distinction between the means of production and the social forces of history. There is a dynamic similarity, too, inasmuch as the internal rearrangements of the elements of the linguistic system are the result of neither purely intellectual nor purely molecular changes, but occur through existential modifications in the same community which is polarized by the desire to establish an intersubjective basis of human action and expression.

Once we have located all institutions, politics, religion, kinship and technology, in their proper cultural or symbolic space,[20] it becomes possible to inquire into the relationships between them and the meaning which persists through them. The method of such a study has been outlined in Max Weber's phenomenology of the "affinity" of the institutions of religion and economics within the matrix defined by the historical *choices* of the Calvinist ethic and the "rationalization" of capitalism. Weber's notion of an "affinity of choices" (*Wahlverwandtschaft*) is the intuition of a certain intelligible transition between the Calvinist transformation of nature to the glory of God and the "rationalization" of labor in capitalist enterprise. Calvinist consciousness oscil-

20. Thomas Langan, *Merleau-Ponty's Critique of Reason* (New Haven and London: Yale University Press, 1966), pp. 42–59.

lates between boundless guilt and utter vindication, just as capitalism is haunted by scarcity and glut. In each case, the flight into materialism results in a total loss of transcendence, vindicated as demystification which is also disenchantment (*Entzauberung*). It becomes possible to understand the solidarity of the orders of economics, politics and religion as a value-additive rather than causal phenomenon once we treat the economic order itself as a choice of social and physical relations. It is then possible, given other preconditions, to see the capitalist system outlined in the Calvinist ethic and the Protestant reformation in the program of capitalist rationalizations. The course of history also illuminates the nature of these fundamental choices. "What we assume in order to understand history is that freedom understands the uses of freedom." [21] The Calvinist juxtaposition of the finite and the infinite, at the same time blocking access to the other world, organized an obsession with this world. While we have no reasons for saying that history will solve this uneasiness, we can struggle to renew the demands of transcendence abolished in the capitalist world which only reveals that the question of transcendence has been poorly posed rather than eliminated.

Finally, it is unnecessary to reject either Marxian or Freudian explanations of history as fallacious reductions of a phenomenologically richer reality since neither is tied to causal language. His-

21. "The Crisis of the Understanding," in *The Primacy of Perception*, p. 204.

torical materialism consists as much in translating
economics into an historical matrix as in bringing
economics into history. This is because the Marxian
conception of economics is not a closed system of
objective facts, but a living cohesion of the material
and social forces of production which is simultaneously an institutional and psychological formation.
Historical materialism takes into account the objective framework of individual action in order to acti-
vate the latent structures of human relationships
which generate the norms of collective existence.
Such an interpretation is not an attempt to spiritual-
ize history in a Hegelian fashion. Economic life is
already transcendent in a confused way just as transcendence in human terms is already the demand
for *a certain* type of economy. "Precisely because
economics is not a closed world, and because all
motivations intermingle at the core of history, the
external becomes internal, and the internal external, and no constituent of our existence can ever be
outrun." [22] Through language we first encounter that
system of exchanges between consciousness and the
world in which meaning is established and renewed
in a permutation of the given and the possible
which offers a paradigm of all cultural institutions,
for it is the matrix of the acquisition and renewal of
the tradition of humanity in each of us. Language,
like other cultural institutions, is often regarded as
a tool or an instrument of thought. But then language is a tool which accomplishes far more and is

22. *Phenomenology of Perception*, p. 172.

far less logical than we might like it to be. It is full of ambiguity and in general far too luxuriant for the taste of positivist philosophers. As a tool, language seems to use us as much as we use it; and in this it is more like the rest of our general culture, which we cannot use without inhabiting it. Ultimately, language, like culture, defeats any attempt to conceive it as a system capable of revealing the genesis of its own meaning. This is because we *are* the language we are talking about. That is to say, we are the material truth of language through our body, which is a natural language. It is through our body that we can speak of the world because the world in turn speaks to us through the body.

Since human perception falls upon a world in which we are enclosed our expression of the world in language and art can never be a simple introduction to the prose of the world apart from its poetry. We express the world through the poetics of our being-in-the-world, beginning with the first act of perception which brings into being the perspective of form and ground through which the invisible and ineffable speaks and becomes visible in us. All other cultural gestures are continuous with the first institution of human labor, speech and art through which the world takes root in us. In this sense, we may consider talk, reading, writing and love as institutions, that is to say, polarizations of the established and the new. We may, for example, distinguish between the institution of *language*, as an objective structure studied by linguistics, and *speech,* which is the use-value language acquires when turned toward expression and the institution of new meanings. We start by reading an author, leaning at first upon the common associations of his words until, gradually, the words begin to flow in us and to open us to an original sound which is the writer's voice borrowing from us an understanding that until then we did not know was ours to offer. Yet it comes only from what we ourselves brought to the book, our knowledge of the language, of ourselves, and of life's questions, which we share with the author. Once we have acquired the author's style of thinking, our lives interweave in a presence that is the anticipation of the whole of the author's intention and its simultaneous recovery which continues the understanding. In talking and listening to one another we make an accommodation through language and the body in which we grow older together. We encroach upon one another and borrow from each other's time, words, and looks what we are looking for in ourselves. In this way our mind and self may be thought of as institutions which we inhabit with others in a system of presences which includes Socrates or Sartre just as much as our friends in the room.

> When I speak or understand, I experience that presence of others in myself or of myself in others which is the stumbling-block of the theory of intersubjectivity, I experience that presence of what is represented which is the stumbling-block of the theory of time, and I finally understand what is meant by Husserl's

enigmatic statement, "Transcendental subjectivity is intersubjectivity." To the extent that what I say has meaning, I am a different "other" for myself when I am speaking; and to the extent that I understand, I no longer know who is speaking and who is listening.[23]

Through language I discover myself and others, in talking, listening, reading and writing. It is language which makes possible that aesthetic distance between myself and the world through which I can speak about the world and the world in turn can speak through me. Our thoughts and purposes are embodied in bodily gestures which in the act of expression structure themselves toward habit and spontaneity; and thus we make our world. Finally, what we may learn from Merleau-Ponty's approach to the phenomenology of language is that expression is always an act of self-improvisation in which we borrow from the world, from others, and from our own past efforts. Language is the child in us which speaks of the world in order to know who he is.

23. *Signs*, p. 97.

6 / Between Montaigne and Machiavelli

MERLEAU-PONTY'S POLITICAL EXPERIENCE is inseparable from the philosophical reflections in which he sought to express the irreducible ambiguity of thought becoming action and the blindness of action unclarified by critical thought. His meditations are identical with political action because they responded to the political situation of his time. Our politics has failed to acquire a voice of its own in which the call to freedom and intersubjectivity eschews the sterile alternatives of anticommunism and anticapitalism. History it seems has played upon politics the same trick that politics hoped to play upon history. The Right and the Left have failed either to stabilize or to put an end to history. Rather, each has acquired a history which includes the other. Capitalism has its future in socialism, but not by any inevitable path. Socialism, however, has its past in capitalism and is more likely to resemble capitalism than to differ from it, if all that lies between them is a vocabulary of freedom lacking an infrastructure of intersubjectivity. Thus neither the Left nor the Right possesses the truth though neither is false, except as each attempts to stand outside of the other, thereby separating itself from its own history and its anchorage in a common political tradition.

Merleau-Ponty would certainly have merited all the anger, if not the awe, of his political friends and opponents had he simply found a position of political skepticism from which to expose the contradictions of the Right and the Left.[1] He knew well enough that in contemporary politics criticism of the Left is tantamount to support of the Right. Yet he could not accept that criticism of the Right meant unqualified support of the Left. This was not because Merleau-Ponty lacked political will-power or wished to indulge the rationalism of the professional intellectual. He might have chosen silence, but he thought of silence as an originary mode of

1. Georg Lukács touches the issue most closely in his criticisms of the inadequacy of Merleau-Ponty's existentialist concept of opinion and its dialectical relation to objective social and historical processes. Lukács' conclusion is that Merleau-Ponty's existentialism, despite its more concrete approach to politics, ultimately falls into eclecticism and nihilism. Cf. *Existentialisme ou Marxisme?* (Paris: Nagel, 1948), pt. 3, chap. 5. My remarks, though not directed at Lukács' criticism, would, I think, answer it as well as give some idea of the rather special sense that Merleau-Ponty gives to the existentialist perspective.

expression in which meaning is fermented and solicited by the world to which it belongs. It might be
mentioned that he had fought beside his fellow
men, that he never ceased to argue with them, to
write for them, to assume their situation as his own.
But this would only add to the enigma of the
distance which men felt between Merleau-Ponty and
themselves. Moreover, it would be wrong to explain
away that distance by an appeal to instances of
comradeship. This would be to fail to see that the
world and others are present to us through an *aesthetic distance* which permits us to inhabit the
world and to encroach upon others without shifting
our own ground. It is this very distance that is the
presupposition of all secondary structures of physical and social existence. Thus Merleau-Ponty established in himself the wonder that men have for each
other but which they mistake for skepticism in those
individuals who excel in that wonder.

It is understandable then that Merleau-Ponty's
political meditations drew inspiration from Montaigne and Machiavelli and that in reflecting upon
them he sought to unravel the ambiguities of skepticism, humanism, and terror in order to clarify that
"astonishing junction between fact and meaning,
between my body and myself, myself and others, my
thought and my speech, violence and truth" which is
the originary ground of social and political life.

I shall attempt to interpret Merleau-Ponty's conception of the ambiguity of politics developed in the

essay *Humanism and Terror* [2] by situating that
essay between his meditations on Montaigne [3] and
Machiavelli. [4] It is hoped that these reflections illu-
minate the larger essay inasmuch as they reveal
Merleau-Ponty's conception of political reflection
and save it from criticisms of skepticism and noncommitment which I think quite alien to Merleau-
Ponty's philosophical thought.

On reading Montaigne it is not enough simply to
say of him that he was a skeptic. For skepticism has
two aspects. It means that nothing is true, but also
that nothing is false. Thus we cannot conclude that
skepticism abandons us to an utter relativism of
truth. Rather, it opens us to the idea of a totality of
truth in which contradiction is a necessary element
in our experience of truth. Montaigne's skepticism is
rooted in the paradox of *conscious being*, to be con-
stantly involved in the world through perception,
politics or love and yet always at a distance from it
without which we would know nothing of it. *"What
is taken to be rare about Perseus King of Macedonia
—that his mind attached itself to no rank but went
wandering through all kinds of life and represent-
ing customs to itself which were so vagabond and
flighty that it was not known to himself or others
what man this was—seems to me more or less to
apply to everyone. We are always thinking some-*

2. *Humanism and Terror, An Essay on the Communist
Problem,* trans. with notes by John O'Neill (Boston: Beacon
Press, 1969).
3. "Reading Montaigne," in *Signs,* pp. 198–210.
4. "A Note on Machiavelli," in *ibid.,* pp. 211–23.

where else." [5] And, as Merleau-Ponty adds, "it could not possibly be otherwise. To be conscious is, among other things, to be somewhere else." Thus the skeptic only withdraws from the world, its passions and follies, in order to find himself at grips with the world, having as it were merely slackened the intentional ties between himself and the world in order to comprehend the paradox of his being-in-the-world. Whenever Montaigne speaks of man he refers to him as "strange," "monstrous," or "absurd." What he has in mind is the paradoxical mixture that we are of mind and body, so that a prince can kill his beloved brother because of a dream he has had.

The variety of human practices produces in Montaigne something more than anthropological curiosity or philosophical skepticism. *"I study myself more than other subjects. It is my metaphysics and my physics."* Because of the mixture of being that he is, the explanation of man can only be given by himself to himself, through an experience of the problematic nature that he is. Man does not borrow himself from philosophy or from science. He is the treasure upon which the sciences draw. Nevertheless, man has to make his own fortune and in this the folly of a treasure laid up in a religious heaven is no better, nor for that matter any worse, than the treasures of Eldorado. For the enthusiasm of religion is a mode of our folly and our folly is essential to us. "When we put not self-satisfied understanding

5. The italicized quotations are cited by Merleau-Ponty from Montaigne's essays, book III.

but a consciousness astonished at itself at the core of human existence, we can neither obliterate the dream of an other side of things nor repress the wordless invocation of this beyond." [6]

Montaigne can, however, speak as though we should remain indifferent to the world and in love or politics never allow ourselves to play more than a role. *"We must lend ourselves to others and give ourselves only to ourselves."* And yet we must adopt the principles of family and state institutions for they are the essential follies of life with others. To attempt to live outside of the state and the family reveals the abstraction of the stoic distinction between what is internal and what is external, between necessity and freedom. "We cannot always obey if we despise, or despise always if we obey. There are occasions when to obey is to accept and to despise is to refuse, when a life which is in part a double life ceases to be possible, and there is no longer any distinction between exterior and interior. Then we must enter the world's folly, and we need a rule for such a moment." [7] But this is not a desperate attempt to achieve certainty. It would only be this if we assumed the standpoint of a finished truth toward which we could move from doubt only by a leap. But that would be to exchange our nature for some other existence, whether animal or angel; *"the extinction of a life is the way to a thousand lives."* If we abandon such a notion then we come back to the

6. *Signs*, p. 203.
7. *Ibid.*, p. 205.

ground of opinion, to the fact that there is truth and men have to learn doubt. *"I know what it is to be human better than I know what it is to be animal, mortal or rational."* Skepticism with respect to the passions only deprives them of value if we assume a total self-possession, whereas we are never wholly ourselves but always interested in the world through the passions which we are. Then we understand the passions as the vehicle by which truth and value are given to us and we see that the critique of the passions is the rejection of false passions which do not carry us toward the world and men, but close us in a subjectivity we have not freely chosen.

While it is the evil of public life to associate us with opinions and projects we have not chosen for ourselves, the flight into the self only reveals the self as openness toward the world and men so that among other things we are for others and their opinion touches the very core of our being.

> The fact of the matter is that true skepticism is movement toward the truth, that the critique of passions is hatred of false passions, and finally, that in *some* circumstances Montaigne recognized outside himself men and things he never dreamed of refusing himself to, because they were like the emblem of his outward freedom, and because in loving them he was himself and regained himself in them as he regained them in himself.[8]

Skepticism and misanthropy whatever the appearances, are misbegotten political virtues for the rea-

8. *Ibid.*, p. 207.

son that the essential ambiguity of politics is that its vices derive from what is most valuable to men— the idea of a truth which each intends for all because men do not live side by side like pebbles, but each lives in all. It is the evidence of the vital truths which men hold intersubjectively which provides the infrastructure of social and political life. This is not to say that this prepolitical suffrage ever exists in abstraction from political and social institutions, nor to deny that it is weighted by ideology. Our task is to make it function as the *norm* of political society, to communicate it through criticism, information, and publicity. This is a difficult task and one which demands a philosophy which is free of political responsibilities because it has its own. Such a philosophy can be free and faithful because it does not play at reconstructing politics, passions, and life, but devotes itself to the disclosure of the basic meaning-structures through which we inhabit the world.

Merleau-Ponty's essay on *Humanism and Terror* is an exercise in political philosophy which is true to itself as philosophy because it dwells within the problematic of communism and anticommunism in order to reveal the latent structures of political action, truth, and violence, which are the foundations of all social existence. The starting point of Merleau-Ponty's reflections on the Communist problem, as it is raised by the Moscow Trials, seems to defeat all progress in the argument and almost ensured that it would win converts from neither side. The

argument runs the risk of being dismissed for its
hesitation, its noncommitment, or even flatly rejected as an ill-timed invitation to skepticism at a
moment when the Third World seems bent upon
learning the ideologies of the Right or the Left. And
yet it is precisely to the problem of the genesis of
political community and the clarification of the historical option which it involves that the essay on
humanism and terror addresses itself. It cannot
therefore be dismissed as a local tract nor be ig-
nored by those whose hope is for an end of
ideology.[9]

"Communism does not invent violence, it finds it
established." Communism has no monopoly on violence. All political regimes are criminal, however
liberal the principles to which they subscribe. Liberal societies are compatible with domestic and international exploitation in which their principles of
freedom and equality participate as mystifications.
The liberal cannot salve his conscience with the
myth that violence has been completely legalized in

9. The following comment upon Arthur Koestler's *Dark-
ness at Noon,* to which *Humanism and Terror* is also a response, seems to be true for both works: "I fancy that this
novel has fallen under a temporary cloud. That is partly
because it is political, and because it was inspired by the
Moscow Trials the butterflies of criticism imagine that it
can be tucked away in the file marked 'Topical.' It was
topical, is topical and always will be topical for in no fore-
seeable future will the circumstance that gave rise to it be
eliminated. It will remain topical just as *Gulliver's Travels*
has remained topical for those who have discovered it is
not just a children's book" (John Atkins, *Arthur Koestler*
[New York: Roy Publishers, 1956], pp. 177–78).

his own society and for that reason he cannot iden-
tify terror with communism. But the Communist
sympathizer is in no better position. Violence cannot
be understood historically or statistically. The death
of a single individual is sufficient to condemn an
entire regime. "The anticommunist refuses to see
that violence is universal, the exalted sympathizer
refuses to see that no one can look violence in the
face." [10] The nature of political action is not con-
tained by the alternatives of the yogi and the commissar, for men are neither entirely interior beings
nor wholly the objects of external manipulation.
This is not to deny that Rubashov might provide
himself with the objectivist arguments of Marxian
scientism and historicism. From this point of view
the self remains an empty category until the party
has fulfilled its historical task of providing the economic infrastructure of authentic subjectivity. But
this is a position motivated by a conception of consciousness as either everything or nothing. Even if
we understand this alternation simply as a political
strategy, the question arises: What does Rubashov
make of his personal consciousness in the days after
the trial when, after publicly saving his past, he is
faced with the existential difference between the
judgment of universal history and his own self-es-
teem? To answer this question we must understand
something of the relation between political reason
and political passions.

"One does not become a revolutionary through

10. *Humanism and Terror*, p. 2.

science, but out of indignation. Science comes afterwards in order to fill in and determine that empty protestation." [11] Rubashov and his comrades had started from the evident truth of the value of men and only later learned that in the course of building its economic infrastructure they would have to subject individuals to the violence generated in the distance between the specific circumstances of the revolution and its future. The paradox of the revolutionary is that the recognition of the value of intersubjectivity engages a struggle to the death which reproduces the alienation of the individual between the options of a subjectivism and an objectivism neither of which can reach its proper conclusion. Marxism does not create this dilemma, it merely expresses it. Koestler, on the other hand, poses the problem in such a way that he neglects what is *moral* in the Marxist decision to treat the self solely from outside, from the standpoint of the objective requirements of history. He thereby misses the essential ambiguity of the distinction between the subjective and the objective standpoints. The values of the yogi are not simply the reverse of those of the commissar because each experiences an internal reversal of the values of subjectivism and objectivism whenever either standpoint is assumed as an absolute. We can understand then that, once in prison, Rubashov experiences the value of the self in the depths of its interiority where it opens toward the White Guard in the neighboring cell *as*

11. *Ibid.,* p. 11.

someone to whom one can talk.[12] The tapping on the prison walls is the first institution of that communication between men for the sake of which Rubashov had embarked upon his revolutionary career. Between the beginning and the end of his life there is, however, a continuity which is possible only through the contradiction which it embraces.

It is this openness toward its own past and future that prevents political action from ever being unequivocal. Hence the historical responsibility that the revolutionary assumes can never be established as a matter of brute fact. The Trials therefore never go beyond the level of a "ceremony of language" in which meaning is sensed entirely within the verbal exchanges and not through reference to an external ground of verification.

> The Trials do not go beyond the subjective and never approach what one calls "true" justice, objective and timeless, *because they bear upon facts which are still open toward the future, which consequently are not yet univocal and only acquire a definitively criminal character when they are viewed from the perspective on the future held by the men in power.*[13]

What the Trials reveal to us is the form and style of the revolutionary. The revolutionary judges what exists in terms of what is to come, he regards the future as more vital than the present to which it owes its birth. From this perspective there can be no subjective honor; we are entirely and solely what we

12. *Ibid.*, p. 5.
13. *Ibid.*, p. 27.

are for others and our relation to them. The revolutionary masters the present in terms of the future, whereas the counterrevolutionary binds the present to the past. The revolutionary shares in an intersubjective conviction of making history—which is, of course, an arbitrary conviction, but with respect to the *future* of which we cannot in principle be certain. However, the evidence of the value of a future society of comrades suffices for a revolutionary decision and its lack of certainty has nothing to do with the individual hesitation that belongs to prerevolutionary sensibilities. For the revolutionary there exists no margin of indifference; political differences are acts of objective treason. In such circumstances government is terror and humanism [14] is suspended. It is this state of affairs which arouses the greatest offense.

The liberal conscience rejects the barbarism of communism. But this amounts to nothing more than a refusal to give violence its name. Civilization is threatened as much by the nameless violence institutionalized in liberal society as it is by terror exercised openly in the hope of putting an end to the history of violence. In the liberal ideology, justice and politics assume a division of labor between concern for ends and the calculation of means. But this is an abstraction from political reality where conflict

14. "There is no serious humanism except the one which looks for man's effective recognition by his fellow man throughout the world. Consequently, it could not possibly precede the moment when humanity gives itself its means of communication and communion" (*Signs*, p. 222).

is generated in the definition of ends because this activity determines what shall be identified as means. In other words questions of justice are identified in terms of so-called abstract values. In reality, truth and justice are inseparable from the violence of possession and dispossession. This is evident in every revolutionary situation where society cannot be assumed but has yet to emerge from its origins in "the passional and illegal origins of all legality and reason," [15] where for a time humanism is suspended precisely because it is in genesis.

It is the problem of the genesis of collective life which is the fundamental theme of Merleau-Ponty's reflections upon the ambiguity of humanism and terror in revolutionary societies. But, of course, he is not dealing here with the fiction of a presocial state of nature introduced in order to rationalize revolt or order according to whether the presocial condition of man is pictured as benign or brutish. Indeed, it is just these alternatives which are not open in the state of nature because it is a genetic state in which violence and justice, truth and contradiction are the very matrix from which the option of a specific historical form of society emerges. Marxists themselves lose sight of the essential contingency in the genesis of a revolutionary praxis to the extent that they treat history as an object of knowledge, ignoring their own attempt to *make* history. The Marxist intervention in history inserts into history a norm of intersubjectivity generated through the very conflict

15. *Humanism and Terror,* p. 37.

and contingency which a scientific law of history seeks to eliminate.

At the same time Merleau-Ponty does not intend to conclude that history is simply a field of radically contingent action—"this irrationalism is indefensible for the decisive reason that *no one lives it, not even he who professes it.*" [16] That the whole of reality for man is only probable whether in the appearance of things or of the future does not mean that the world lacks a style of physiognomy in its appearance to us. We live in subjective certainties which we intend universally and practically and that are in no way illusory unless we posit some apodictic certainty outside the grounds of human experience. "The future is only probable, but it is not an empty zone in which we can construct gratuitous projects; it is sketched before us like the beginning of the day's end, and its outline is ourselves." [17] We do not experience uncertainty at the very core of our existence. The center of our experience is a common world in which we make appraisals, enlist support, and seek to convince our opponents, never doubting the potential permutation of subjective and objective evidence.

While it is true that our perspectives depend upon our motives and values, it is just as true that our values are derived from concrete experience and not drawn from some pre-established sphere. Thus contradiction and conflict do not stem from ab-

16. *Ibid.*, p. 95.
17. *Ibid.*

stractly opposed principles or perspectives but presuppose a fundamental community of experience which gives meaning to such conflict. "The dialectic of the subjective and objective is not a simple contradiction which leaves the terms it plays on disjointed; it is rather a testimony to our rootedness in the truth." [18] This fundamental ambiguity of truth and contradiction, far from being destructive of intersubjectivity, in fact presupposes a community of men as its originary ground. This presupposition differs from the liberal assumption of a finished human nature. In terms of the latter it is impossible to understand conflict and error as anything but historical accidents, rather than as elements in a matrix from which truth and community emerge. Marxism differs from liberalism and anarchism [19] in that it can account for violence in history, not in the

18. *Ibid.*, p. 96.

19. "Here we are not speaking in favor of an anarchical liberty: if I wish freedom for another person it is inevitable that even this wish will be seen by him as an alien law; and so liberalism turns into violence. One can only blind oneself to this outcome by refusing to reflect upon the relation between the self and others. The anarchist who closes his eyes to this dialectic is nonetheless exposed to its consequences. It is the basic fact on which we have to build freedom. We are not accusing liberalism of being a system of violence, we reproach it with not seeing its own face in violence, with veiling the pact upon which it rests while rejecting as barbarous that other source of freedom—revolutionary freedom—which is the origin of all social pacts. With the assumptions of impersonal Reason and rational Man, and by regarding itself as a natural rather than an historical fact, liberalism assumes universality as a datum whereas the problem is its realization in the dialectic of concrete intersubjectivity" (*ibid.*, p. 35, n. 11).

sense of providing it with excuses but in the sense that it situates violence within the ambiguous origins of truth and justice, in the birth of reason from unreason that is the mark of a new society. The notions of truth and freedom arise only in certain cultures and are not historical laws as is pretended in the liberal version of history. Truth and freedom are options of history whose matrix is violence. The option which history opens up for us is ourselves and this option remains irreducibly what it is whether we contemplate it as a spectacle or implement it through action.

The foundations of history and politics are inseparable from the dialectic between man and nature and between man and his fellow men. It is the nature of human consciousness to realize itself in the world and among men and its embodiment is the essential mode of its opening toward the world and to others. The problem of community and coexistence only arises for an embodied consciousness driven by its basic needs into a social division of labor and engaged by its deepest need in a life and death struggle for intersubjective recognition. Embodied consciousness never experiences an original innocence to which any violence would be an irreparable harm; it knows only different kinds of violence. For consciousness finds itself already engaged in the world, in definite situations in which its resources are never merely its own but derive from the exploitation of its position as the husband of this woman, the child of these parents, the master of these slaves. As such the intentions of embodied consciousness already presuppose a common matrix of justice and injustice, truth and deception, out of which they emerge as acts of love, hate, honesty, and deceit. This is the ground presupposed by political discussion and political choice. We never act upon isolated individuals, as the liberal imagines, but always within a community which possesses a common measure of the good and evil it knows. As soon as we have lived we already know what it means for subjects to treat one another as objects, placing into jeopardy the community of subjectivity which is the originary goal of embodied consciousness. None of us reaches manhood outside of this history of the violence we hold for one another. None of us can bear it apart from the attempt within this violence to establish love and communion.

The prospects of humanism are wholly bound up with the *meaning* which Marxism introduces into violence as a polarity within a structure of truth and intersubjectivity against which all other forms of violence are retrograde. But the norm of intersubjectivity is not itself a law of history and its own genesis has no guarantee precisely because it lies in the revelation of man to himself and finds, as it were, its natural limit in man. The attempt to establish harmony within ourselves and with others as an existential truth is not routed by conflict and error, but assumes them as something we can overcome as fellow men.

This last reflection raises once again the question of the relation between truth and community. The problem is that the emergence of truth seems to presuppose a community, and in turn the emergence of a community assumes a concept of truth. The Marxist criticism of the liberal truth lies in the exposition of its lack of correspondence with the objective relations between men in liberal society. The problem of communism is similar, since it has failed so far to make the historical road-repairs which were written into its political charter. Marxism claims to be a truth in the making; it overturns liberal society in order to clear the way for the genesis of a society grounded in authentic intersubjectivity. The birth of Communist society, however, is no less painful than the birth of man himself, and already from the earliest years it is familiar with violence and contradiction.

Merleau-Ponty's thought dwells within the circle of this problem and it seems natural that he should have turned toward Machiavelli whose own meditations embraced the same problematic. "For he describes that knot of collective life in which pure morality can be cruel and pure politics requires something like a morality." [20] Had either Montaigne or Machiavelli stood outside of politics in order to contemplate political action, then they might easily have succumbed to the conclusions of skepticism and cynicism. But then they would have broken the circle of being which we inhabit whereas they chose

20. *Signs,* p. 211.

to dwell and to meditate within it. They would not otherwise have provided a model for Merleau-Ponty's reflections upon their experience, which, we suggest, is indirectly his own political experience.

If the cynic is right and humanity essentially an accident, then it is difficult to see what else besides sheer force could uphold collective life. In this mood Machiavelli is obsessed with violence and oppression. But there is a deeper reflection in Machiavelli which discovers something other than sheer force in the phenomenon of conflict and aggression. "While men are trying not to be afraid, they begin to make themselves feared by others; and they transfer to others the aggression that they push back from themselves, as if it were absolutely necessary to offend or be offended." [21] Human aggression is not simply a conflict of animal or physical forces, but a polarity within a dialectic of intersubjective recognition or alienation. Political power never rests upon naked force but always presumes a ground of opinion and consensus within a margin of potential conflict and violence that is crossed only when this common sense is outraged. "Relationships between the subject and those in power, like those between the self and others, are cemented at a level deeper than judgment. As long as it is not a matter of the radical challenge of contempt, they survive challenge." [22] The exercise of power succeeds best as an appeal to freedom rather than as an act of violence

21. *Ibid.*, p. 211–12.
22. *Ibid.*, p. 213.

which only reinforces itself through the aggression which it arouses. The art of the Prince is to maintain the free consent of his subjects and in this we discover a touchstone for a humanist politics inasmuch as the people at least seek to avoid oppression if not to aim at anything greater.

The *virtue* of the Prince is a mode of living with others such that their opinion is consulted without being followed slavishly nor merely heard without effect. At such times there is always the possibility that the originary conflict of will and opinion will arise and yet it is only under these conditions that there can be genuine consultation and real leadership. Within such a community the exercise of power is tied to the realm of appearances, for only the Prince can know how the people are and only they know him.

> What sometimes transforms softness into cruelty and harshness into value, and overturns the precepts of private life, is that acts of authority intervene in a certain state of opinion which changes their meaning. They awake an echo which is at times immeasurable. They open or close hidden fissures in the block of general consent, and trigger a molecular process which may modify the whole course of events. Or as mirrors set around in a circle transform a slender flame into a fairyland, acts of authority reflected in the constellation of consciousness are transfigured, and the reflections of these reflections create an appearance which is the proper place—the truth, in short—of historical action.[23]

23. *Ibid.*, p. 216.

Machiavelli is a difficult thinker because he forces upon us the ambiguity of virtue from which self-styled humanists so often shrink, preferring the history of principles to the history of men. Between Montaigne, Machiavelli and Marx, on the other hand, there is common effort to consider the nature of history and politics within the boundaries that men set for themselves. That is to say, human action always achieves something more and something less than it envisages and yet political man must assume the consequences. Far from being a fatal flaw in the nature of action this essential ambiguity is what makes human actions neither blindly impulsive nor divinely efficacious. At the same time, the ambiguity of political action is not a justification for the lack of political conviction or fidelity. For what introduces ambiguity into political action is precisely the metamorphoses of truth and justice experienced in putting them into practice without any absolute guarantee that this project will not be attacked, sabotaged and even undermined from within. It is, in short, the denial of political innocence even at the birth of freedom.

Finally, Merleau-Ponty teaches us the lesson that truth and justice are alien to history and politics in the sense that they can never be completely realized and yet never exist entirely apart from the life and vicissitudes of community and power. The expression of truth and justice is never a solitary confrontation of the philosopher and a truth which he expresses, unless we lose sight of the community

to which the philosopher belongs and before whom
he expresses the truth. This is not to say that the
philosopher expresses the truth solely in accordance
with others, any more than for himself alone, or as
the voice of a truth in itself in abstraction from
himself and others. The enigma of philosophy is
that sometimes life has the *same* face for us and for
others and before the truth, so that the philosopher
is called to share a life whose truth and goodness is
evident and he would never think of opposing himself to his fellow men or setting truth against life.
And yet the philosopher knows the limits of other
men and must refuse them, but with all the more
peace that comes from sharing the same world.
"Hence the rebellious gentleness, the thoughtful ad-
herence, the intangible presence that upset those
around him." [24]

To pose the problem of truth and opinion in this
way opens memory to what is close to us from the
past and lends immediacy to the life and death of
Socrates who bore men the same love that he bore
towards philosophy. If Socrates had simply denied
the gods of the City he would have shown his fellow
men nothing more than their daily practice. But
Socrates sacrificed to the gods and obeyed the law of
the City to his death. Or if Socrates had claimed to
believe more than his fellow men he might well
have scandalized them; but in either case, whether
through excess or revolt, he would not have conveyed his essential irony, which is to have thought

24. *Éloge de la philosophie*, p. 41.

religion true but not in the way it understood itself to be true, just as he believed the *polis* to be just but not for reasons of state. Socrates could speak as though he obeyed the laws out of the conservatism of age and the gradualism it calls hope. But his inertia is more truly that of his daimon or the absolute standpoint of an internal truth which admonishes through joining man to his own ignorance. Only by engaging his judges in the example of an obedience which is simultaneously a resistance, in an encounter with a truth which is proved whether they sentence him or acquit him can Socrates introduce into the *polis* the principle of philosophy which transforms the certainty of religion by bringing both religion and philosophy to the same ground. Thus the Socratic irony does not lie in the exploitation of the differences of level between philosophy and religion but in the experience of their reversal. The significance of Socrates' obedience to the laws is that henceforth the *polis* is the guardian of the individual soul; it has become a citadel without walls and hence no longer needs the laws of religion and the state—it needs men.

There is no complacency or self-sufficiency behind the Socratic irony. "The irony of Socrates is a distant but true relation with others. It expresses the fundamental fact that each of us is himself only when there is no escape and yet can recognize himself in the other. It is an attempt to release us together for freedom." [25] There would be no tragedy

25. *Ibid.*, p. 47.

in Socrates' stand before the Athenian Assembly if he had not believed that his fellow men could understand him or that no one after him would take a similar stand. Not everyone voted to condemn Socrates; for truth and error, justice and injustice are never whole and have always to be taken up again in every age and by every man. It is the same faith which inspired Merleau-Ponty's meditations on the true distance which is the source of meaning and poetry within the fold and flesh of the world.

Bibliography

[1]   WORKS BY MAURICE MERLEAU-PONTY

Les Aventures de la dialectique. Paris: Gallimard, 1955.
[Article in] *The Bergsonian Heritage,* edited by Thomas
    Hanna. New York: Columbia University Press, 1962.
"Cinq notes sur Claude Simon." *Médiations,* IV (1961),
    5–10.
Éloge de la philosophie et autres essais. Paris: Galli-
    mard, 1960.
*Éloge de la philosophie: Leçon inaugurale faite au Col-
    lège de France, le jeudi 15 Janvier 1953.* Paris: Galli-
    mard, 1953.
*Humanisme et terreur, essai sur le probleme commu-
    niste.* Paris: Gallimard, 1947.
"Husserl et la notion de nature (Notes prises au cours
    de Maurice Merleau-Ponty)." Two lectures given
    March 14 and 25, 1957, transcribed by Xavier Til-
    liette. *Revue de métaphysique et de morale,* LXX
    (1965), 257–69.

"Un inédit de Maurice Merleau-Ponty." With an introduction by Martial Gueroult. *Revue de métaphysique et de morale,* LXVII (1962), 401–9.

L'Œil et l'esprit. Paris: Gallimard, 1964.

"Pages d' 'Introduction à la prose du monde' [presentées par Claude Lefort]." *Revue de métaphysique et de morale,* LXXII (1967), 139–53.

Phénoménologie de la perception. Paris: Gallimard, 1945.

Les Philosophes célèbres, with Ferdinand Alquie, *et al.* Paris: L. Mazenod, 1956.

"La Philosophie de l'existence." *Dialogue,* V (1966), 307–22.

La Prose du monde. Edited by Claude Lefort. Paris: Gallimard, 1969.

Les Relations avec autrui chez l'enfant: Introduction. Paris: Centre de documentation universitaire, 1958.

Résumés de cours, Collège de France, 1952–1960. Paris: Gallimard, 1968.

Les Sciences de l'homme et la phénoménologie. Paris: Centre de documentation universitaire, 1958.

Sens et non-sens. Paris: Nagel, 1948.

Signes. Paris: Gallimard, 1960.

La Structure du comportement. Paris: Presses universitaires de France, 1942. 5th edition, preceded by "Une philosophie de l'ambiguïté," by Alphonse de Waelhens, 1963.

L'Union de l'âme et du corps chez Malebranche, Biran et Bergson. Notes prises au cours de Maurice Merleau-Ponty, recueillies et rédigées par Jean Deprun. Paris: J. Vrin, 1968.

Le Visible et l'invisible, suivi de notes de travail. Texte établi par Claude Lefort, accompagné d'un avertissement et d'une postface. Paris: Gallimard, 1964.

[2] TRANSLATIONS OF MERLEAU-PONTY'S WORKS

Humanism and Terror. Translated by John O'Neill. Boston: Beacon Press, 1969.

In Praise of Philosophy. Translated, with a preface by James M. Edie and John Wild. Evanston, Ill.: Northwestern University Press, 1963.

Phenomenology of Perception. Translated by Colin Smith. London: Routledge and Kegan Paul; New York: Humanities Press, 1962.

The Primacy of Perception and Other Essays. Edited by James M. Edie. Evanston, Ill.: Northwestern University Press, 1964.

The Prose of the World. Translated by John O'Neill. Evanston Ill.: Northwestern University Press, forthcoming.

Sense and Non-Sense. Translated by Hubert L. and Patricia A. Dreyfus. Evanston, Ill.: Northwestern University Press, 1964.

Signs. Translated by Richard C. McCleary. Evanston, Ill.: Northwestern University Press, 1964.

The Structure of Behavior. Translated by Alden L. Fisher. Boston: Beacon Press, 1963.

The Visible and the Invisible. Translated by Alphonso Lingis. Evanston, Ill.: Northwestern University Press, 1969.

[3] WORKS ON MERLEAU-PONTY

1. *In English*

Bannan, John F. "The 'Later' Thought of Merleau-Ponty." *Dialogue,* V (1966), 383–403

Bannan, John F. "Merleau-Ponty on God." *International Philosophical Quarterly*, VI (1966), 341–65.

———. *The Philosophy of Merleau-Ponty*. New York: Harcourt, Brace & World, 1967.

Barral, Mary Rose. *Merleau-Ponty: The Role of the Body-Subject in Interpersonal Relations*. Pittsburgh: Duquesne University Press, 1965.

Bayer, Raymond. "Merleau-Ponty's Existentialism." University of Buffalo Studies, vol. XIX, no. 3; Monographs in Philosophy, no. 3, 1951.

Busch, Thomas. "Merleau-Ponty and the Problem of Origins." *Philosophy Today*, XI (1967), 124–30.

Daly, James. "Merleau-Ponty's Concept of Phenomenology." *Philosophical Studies*, XVI (1967), 137–64.

Dreyfus, Hubert L. "The Three Worlds of Merleau-Ponty." *Philosophy and Phenomenological Research*, XXII (1962), 559–65.

Hanly, C. M. T. "Phenomenology, Consciousness and Freedom (Merleau-Ponty)." *Dialogue*, V (1966), 323–45.

Haymond, William S. "Merleau-Ponty on Sensory Perception." *Modern Schoolman*, XLIV (1966–67), 93–111.

Kaelin, Eugene Francis. *An Existentialist Aesthetic: The Theories of Sartre and Merleau-Ponty*. Madison: University of Wisconsin Press, 1962.

Kockelmans, Joseph A. "Merleau-Ponty's Phenomenology of Language." *Review of Existential Psychology and Psychiatry*, III (1963), 39–82.

———. "Merleau-Ponty's View on Space-Perception and Space." *Review of Existential Psychology and Psychiatry*, IV (1964), 69–105.

Kwant, Remy C. *From Phenomenology to Metaphysics: An Inquiry into the Last Period of Merleau-Ponty's Philosophical Life*. Pittsburgh: Duquesne University Press, 1966.

———. "The Human Body as the Self-Awareness of Being (An Inquiry into the Last Phase of Merleau-Ponty's Philosophical Life)." *Review of Existential Psychology and Psychiatry,* VIII (1968), 117–34.

———. *The Phenomenological Philosophy of Merleau-Ponty.* Pittsburgh: Duquesne University Press, 1963.

Langan, Thomas. "Maurice Merleau-Ponty: In Memoriam." *Philosophy and Phenomenological Research,* XXIII (1962–63), 205–16.

———. *Merleau-Ponty's Critique of Reason.* New Haven: Yale University Press, 1966.

Murphy, Richard T. "A Metaphysical Critique of Method: Husserl and Merleau-Ponty." In *The Quest for the Absolute,* edited by F. J. Adelmann, pp. 175–207. The Hague: Martinus Nijhoff, 1966.

Pietersma, Henry. "Husserl's Concept of Philosophy." *Dialogue,* V (1966), 425–42.

Rabil, Albert. *Merleau-Ponty, Existentialist of the Social World.* New York: Columbia University Press, 1967.

Schmitt, Richard. "Maurice Merleau-Ponty." *Review of Metaphysics,* XIX (1965–66), 492–516, 728–41.

Schrader, George A., ed. *Existential Philosophers: Kierkegaard to Merleau-Ponty.* New York: McGraw-Hill, 1967.

Sheridan, James F. "On Ontology and Politics: A Polemic." *Dialogue,* VII (1968), 449–60.

Smith, Colin. "The Notion of Object in the Phenomenology of Merleau-Ponty." *Philosophy,* XXXIX (1964), 110–19.

Vandenbussche, Frans. "The Problem of God in the Philosophy of Merleau-Ponty." *International Philosophical Quarterly,* VII (1967), 44–67.

Verstraelen, Eugene. "Language Analysis and Merleau-Ponty's Phenomenology of Language." *Saint Louis Quarterly,* IV (1966), 325–42.

Virasoro, Manuel. "Merleau-Ponty and the World of Perception." *Philosophy Today,* III (1959) 66–72.

Zaner, Richard M. "Piaget and Merleau-Ponty: A Study in Convergence." *Review of Existential Psychology and Psychiatry*, VI (1966), 7–23.

————. *The Problem of Embodiment* (The Hague: Martinus Nijhoff, 1964).

2. *In French*

Bayer, Raymond. "Merleau-Ponty et l'existentialisme." *Revue philosophique de la France et de l'étranger*, LXXXVII (1962), 107–17.

Bergeron, André. "La Conscience engagée dans le régime des significations selon Merleau-Ponty." *Dialogue*, V (1966), 373–82.

Cowley, Fraser. "L'Expression et la parole d'après Merleau-Ponty." *Dialogue*, V (1966), 360–72.

Deprun, Jean. *L'Union de l'âme et du corps chez Malebranche, Biran et Bergson: Notes prises au cours de Merleau-Ponty a l'école normale supérieure (1947–1948)*. Paris: J. Vrin, 1968.

Devaux, André A. "Idéalisme critique et positivisme phénoménologique (L'Esquisse d'un dialogue entre M. Joseph Moreau et Maurice Merleau-Ponty)." *Giornale di Metafísica*, XVII (1962), 72–91.

de Waelhens, Alphonse. "In Memoriam Maurice Merleau-Ponty." *Tijdschrift voor Filosofie*, XXIII (1961), 340–47.

————. "Merleau-Ponty, philosophe de la peinture." *Revue de métaphysique et de morale*, LXVII (1962), 431–49.

————. *Une philosophie de l'ambiguïté: L'Existentialisme de Maurice Merleau-Ponty*. Louvain: Publications universitaires de Louvain, 1951. 2d edition; Louvain: Editions Nauwelaerts, 1967.

————. "Situation de Merleau-Ponty." *Les Temps modernes*, XVII, nos. 185–86 (1961), 377–98.

Dufrenne, Mikel. "Les Aventures de la dialectique ou les avatars d'une amitié philosophique (Merleau-Ponty)."

In *Jalons*, by Mikel Dufrenne, pp. 169–73. The Hague: Martinus Nijhoff, 1966.

——. "Maurice Merleau-Ponty." *Les Études philosophiques*, XVII (1962), 81–92.

Fressin, Augustin. *La Perception chez Bergson et chez Merleau-Ponty*. Paris: S.E.D.E.S., 1967.

Gandillac, Maurice de. "Maurice Merleau-Ponty (1908–1961)." *Revue philosophique de la France et de l'étranger*, LXXXVII (1962), 103–6.

Halda, Bernard. *Merleau-Ponty ou la philosophie de l'ambiguïté*. Paris: Les lettres modernes, 1966.

Hyppolite, Jean. "Existence et dialectique dans la philosophie de Merleau-Ponty." *Les Temps modernes*, XVII, nos. 184–85 (1961), 228–44.

——. *Sens et existence dans la philosophie de Maurice Merleau-Ponty*. The Zaharoff Lecture for 1963. Oxford: Clarendon Press, 1963.

Kemp, Peter. "La Philosophie du langage de Merleau-Ponty." *Danish Yearbook of Philosophy*, IV (1967), 7–11.

Lacan, Jacques. "Maurice Merleau-Ponty." *Les Temps modernes*, XVII, nos. 184–85 (1961), 245–54.

Lacroix, Jean. "Un philosophe de l'ambiguïté: Maurice Merleau-Ponty." In *Panorama de la philosophie française contemporaine*, edited by J. Lacroix, pp. 140–47. Paris: Presses universitaires de France, 1966.

Lageux, Maurice. "Merleau-Ponty et la linguistique de Saussure." *Dialogue*, IV (1965–66), 351–64.

——. "Y-a-t-il une philosophie de l'histoire chez Merleau-Ponty?" *Dialogue*, V (1966), 404–17.

Les Temps modernes, XVII, nos. 184–85 (1961), 193–436. Special issue.

Mesaventures de l'anti-marxisme: Les Malheurs de M. Merleau-Ponty par R. Garaudy et al. Avec une lettre de Georg Lukacs. Paris: Éditions sociales, 1956.

Moreau, André. "Merleau-Ponty et Berkeley." *Dialogue*, V (1966), 418–24.

Moreau, Joseph. *L'Horizon des esprits: Essai critique sur la "Phénoménologie de la perception."* Paris: Presses universitaires de France, 1960.

Pariente, Jean-Claude. "Lecture de Merleau-Ponty, I–II [Signes, L'Œil et l'esprit]." *Critique*, XVIII, no. 186 (1962), 957–74; no. 187, 1066–78.

Pontalis, J. B. "Note sur le problème de l'inconscient chez Merleau-Ponty." *Les Temps modernes,* XVII, nos. 184–85 (1961), 287–303.

Racette, Jean. "Le Corps et l'âme, la chair et l'esprit, selon Merleau-Ponty." *Dialogue,* V (1966), 346–59.

Ricoeur, Paul. "Hommage à Merleau-Ponty." *Esprit,* XXIX (1961), 1115–20.

Robinet, André. *Merleau-Ponty: Sa vie, son œuvre, avec un exposé de sa philosophie.* Paris: Presses universitaires de France, 1963.

Sartre, Jean-Paul. "Merleau-Ponty vivant." *Les Temps modernes,* XVII, nos. 184–85 (1961), 304–76.

Szaszkiewicz, Georgius. *Relation entre le comportement et la connaissance selon Merleau-Ponty: Intelligence, liberté et réflexion.* Rome: Tip. P.U.G., 1962.

Thévénaz, Pierre. *De Husserl à Merleau-Ponty: Qu'est-ce que la phénoménologie?* With an introduction by Jean Brun. Neuchâtel: Éditions de la Baconnière, 1966.

Tilliette, Xavier. "Le Corps et le temps dans la 'Phénoménologie de la perception.'" *Studia philosophica,* XXIV (1964), 193–209.

———. "Merleau-Ponty ou la mesure de l'homme." *Archives de philosophie,* XXIV (1961), 399–413.

———. "Une philosophie sans absolu: Maurice Merleau-Ponty, 1908–1961." *Etudes,* CCCX (1961), 215–29.

———. *Philosophes contemporains: Gabriel Marcel, Maurice Merleau-Ponty, Karl Jaspers.* Paris: Desclée de Brouwer, 1962.

van Breda, H. L. "Maurice Merleau-Ponty et les Archives-Husserl à Louvain." *Revue de métaphysique et de morale*, LXVII (1962), 410–30.

3. *In Italian*

Bonomi, Andrea. *Esistenza e struttura: Saggio su Merleau-Ponty*. Milan: Il Saggiatore, 1967.

Capizzi, Antonio. "Figure dell'ateismo francese del dopoguerra [André Gide, Jean-Paul Sartre, Albert Camus, Maurice Merleau-Ponty]." *Giornale critico della filosofia italiana*, XLV (1966), 541–86.

Centineo, Ettore. *Una fenomenologia della storia: L'esistenzialismo di M. Merleau-Ponty*. Palermo: Palumbo, 1959.

Derossi, Giorgio. "Dalla percezione alla visione: L'ontologia negativa dell'ultimo Merleau-Ponty." *Filosofia*, XVI (1965), 333–57.

———. "L'emergenza del percepito e del significato dal progetto intenzionale corporeo in Merleau-Ponty." *Filosofia*, XV (1964), 127–53.

———. *Maurice Merleau-Ponty*. Turin: Edizioni di filosofia, 1965.

———. "Maurice Merleau-Ponty dall'(ambiguità) al trascendentalismo corporeo." *Filosofia*, XIV (1963), 387–411.

———. "Tempo soggetto, cogito e conoscenza intenzionale diretta (non-mediata) in Merleau-Ponty." *Filosofia*, XV (1964), 687–715.

Fausta, Falco. "La fluidificazione dell'assoluto in M. Merleau-Ponty." *Atti dell'Academia delle Scienze di Torino*, VC (1960–61), 66–72.

Ferraris, Anna. "L'apertura all'alterità nella filosofia di Maurice Merleau-Ponty." *Atti dell'Academia delle Scienze di Torino*, XCVII (1962–63), 249–91.

Greppi, Alessandra. "'Le Visible et l'invisible' di M.

Merleau-Ponty." *Rivista di filosofia neo-scolastica,* LIX (1967), 238–44.

"P. P. Merleau-Ponty." *Giornale critico della filosofia italiana,* XLII (1963), 426–27.

Papi, Fulvio. "Libertà e marxismo in Merleau-Ponty." In *Atti del XII Congresso Internazionale di Filosofia* (Venice, September 12–18, 1958), vol. XII, *Storia della filosofia moderna e contemporanea,* pp. 361–68.

Semerari, Giuseppe. *Da Schelling a Merleau-Ponty: Studi sulla filosofia contemporanea.* Bologna: Cappelli, 1962.

Sturani, Enrico. "Letture di Merleau-Ponty." *Rivista di filosofia,* LVIII (1967), 164–82.

4. In Spanish

Blanco, Domingo. "Vida y conocimiento en la filosofía de Merleau-Ponty." *Rivista di filosofia,* XX (1961), 177–95.

Ceriotto, C. L. "Lenguaje y reflexión según Merleau-Ponty." *Philosophia,* no. 29 (1964), 50–58.

Beauvoir, Simone de. *Sartre versus Merleau-Ponty.* Translated by Anibal Leal. Buenos Aires: Ed. Signo Veinte, 1963.

Delfino, R. "Cuerpo alma en Merleau-Ponty." *Ciencia y fe,* XX (1964), 35–76.

Estrabou, Elma. "La significación del tiempo en la filosofía de Merleau-Ponty." *Revista de humanidades,* II (1962), 58–66.

Montull, Tomás. "El atéismo de Merleau-Ponty. *La ciencia tomista,* XC (1963), 115–81.

———. "Maurice Merleau-Ponty y su filosofía." *Estudios filosóficos,* XI (1962), 371–414; XII (1963), 81–133.

———. "Merleau-Ponty: Fenomenología y campo fenoménico." *Estudios filosóficos*, XIII (1964), 41–80.

Ravagnán, Luis María. *Merleau-Ponty.* Buenos Aires: Centro editor de America Latina, 1967.

Touron del Pie, Eliseo. *El hombre el mundo y Dios en la fenomenología de Merleau-Ponty.* Madrid: Revista estudio, 1961.

5. *In Dutch*

Bakker, R. "De geschiedenis in het denken van Merleau-Ponty." *Wijsgerig perspectief de maatschappij en wetenschap*, VI (1965–66), 44–56.

Brus, B. Th. "Een samenvatting van de zlenswijzen van M. Merleau-Ponty met betrekking tot de taal." *Algemeen nederlands tijdschrift voor wijsbegeerte en psychologie. assen.*, LVI (1963–64), 75–87.

Kwant, Remy C. "De autonomie van de wijsbegeerte volgens Merleau-Ponty." *Algemeen nederlands tijdschrift voor wijsbegeerte en psychologie. assen.*, LVIII (1966), 122–35.

———. *De fenomenologie van Merleau-Ponty.* Utrecht: Het Spectrum, 1962.

———. *Mens en expressie in het licht van de wijsbegeerte van Merleau-Ponty.* Utrecht and Antwerp: Aula-Boeken, 1968.

———. "Merleau-Ponty's phaenomenologie van de perceptie." *Wijsgerig perspectief de maatschappij en wetenschap*, II (1961–62), 267–80.

———. "O.E.S.A., In memorium, M. Merleau-Ponty." *Streven*, XIV (1960–61), 946–50.

———. *De stemmen van de stitte: Merleau-Ponty's analyse van de schilderkunst.* Hilversum: Paul Brand, 1966.

———. "De wijsbegeerte van Merleau-Ponty." *Algemeen nederlands tijdschrift voor wijsbegeerte en psychologie. assen.*, LIV (1961–62), 1–21.

——. *De wijsbegeerte van Merleau-Ponty*. 2d edition. Utrecht and Antwerp: Aula-Boeken, 1968.

Strasser, S. "Merleau-Ponty's bijdrage tot de sociaal-filosofie: Interpretatie en critick." *Tijdschrift voor filosofie*, XXIX (1967), 427–65.

van Haecht, L. "In memoriam Maurice Merleau-Ponty (1908–3 mei 1961)." *Dietsche Warande en Belfort*, CVI (1961), 350–53.

6. *In German*

Maier, Willi. *Das Problem der Leiblichkeit bei Jean-Paul Sartre und Maurice Merleau-Ponty*. Tübingen: Max Niemeyer, 1964.

Waldenfels, Bernhard. "Gedenken an Maurice Merleau-Ponty." *Zeitschrift für philosophische Forschung*, XVI (1962), 406–13.

——. "Das Problem der Leiblichkeit bei Merleau-Ponty." *Philosophisches Jahrbuch*, LXXV (1967–68), 347–65.

7. *In Portuguese*

Antunes, M. "Significação de M. Merleau-Ponty." *Brotéria*, LXXIV (1962), 546–60.

Fragata, Júlio. "A filosofia de Merleau-Ponty." *Revista Portuguêsa de filosofia*, XIX (1963), 113–41.

Vita, Luis Washington. "M. Merleau-Ponty (1908–1961), In memoriam." *Revista brasileira de filosofia*, XI (1961), 272–74.